A Bite-Sized Public Affairs Book

V. S. Naipaul:

The Legacy

Edited by
John Mair, Richard Lance Keeble and Farrukh Dhondy

Published by Bite-Sized Books Ltd 2018

Bite-Sized Books Ltd Cleeve Croft, Cleeve Road, Goring RG8 9BJ UK
information@bite-sizedbooks.com
Registered in the UK. Company Registration No: 9395379

Bite-Sized Books Ltd Cleeve Croft, Cleeve Road, Goring RG8 9BJ UK
information@bite-sizedbooks.com
Registered in the UK. Company Registration No: 9395379
ISBN: 9781723774225

Dedication

This book is dedicated to the memory of

Sarah Insanally

(September 12, 1967-September 11, 2018).

Her husband, Riyad, Guyana's Ambassador to the United States and formerly the Organisation of American States' Ambassador to Trinidad, provided much help and inspiration for this book – even in very troubled personal times.

The editors

John Mair

John Mair is one of the most prolific editors of books on modern journalism in Britain today. This publication is his 24th 'hackademic' text; he is currently putting together the 25th – on 'Anti-Social Media'. The books bring together the work of journalists and academics to discuss vital issues such as data journalism, Brexit, Trump and the media, the death of print and the Leveson Inquiry. The genre he invented – with books jointly edited with Richard Tait, Tor Clark, Richard Lance Keeble, Raymond Snoddy and others – is widely recognised as constituting a major addition to contemporary journalism studies. John has practised journalism at the BBC, Channel Four and other broadcasters and taught it at the universities of Coventry, Westminster, Brunel, Kent and Edinburgh Napier. He has judged the British Press Awards, the British Journalism Awards, the Royal Television Society Journalism Awards and helped to set up the Steve Hewlett Memorial Lecture and Scholarships. In September 2018, he was given a Guyana High Commission Award for 'services to the community' i.e. the Guyana diaspora in the UK.

Richard Lance Keeble

Richard Lance Keeble is Professor of Journalism at the University of Lincoln and Visiting Professor at Liverpool Hope University. He is the author and editor of 39 books on a wide range of topics: peace journalism, literary journalism, practical newspaper skills, media ethics, the secret state and the media, profiles, journalism and humour, the coverage of US/UK military adventures and George Orwell. He is joint editor of *Ethical Space: The International Journal of Communication Ethics* and *George Orwell Studies*. In 2011, he gained a National Teaching Fellowship, the highest award for teachers in the UK, and in 2013 the Association for Journalism Education gave him a Lifetime Achievement Award.

Farrukh Dhondy

Farrukh Dhondy is an Indian-born British writer, playwright, screenwriter and left-wing activist of Parsi descent who resides in the United Kingdom. He is well-known not only for his writing but also for his film and TV work. Dhondy's literary output is vast, including books for children, textbooks and biographies, as well as plays for theatre and scripts film and television. He is also a columnist, a biographer (of C. L. R. James, 2001) and media executive, having been a Commissioning Editor at Channel Four from 1984 to 1997. He wrote the comedy series *Tandoori Nights* (1985-1987) for the channel, which concerned the rivalry of two curry house owners. His children's stories include *KBW (Keep Britain White)*, a study of a young white boy's response to anti-Bengali racism. In 2011, Dhondy published his translation of selections from the Sufi poet Jalaluddin Rumi, *Rumi: A New Translation*. He also wrote the screenplay for the Bollywood historical blockbuster *Mangal Pandey*, starring Aamir Khan and Toby Stephens. In 2012, he scripted a short film called *The K File*, a fictional take on the judgement of Ajmal Kasab, directed by Oorvazi Irani. In 2013, his critically acclaimed play *Devdas* was premièred in London and was subsequently replayed globally. 2013 also saw the publication of the novel *Prophet of Love* (HarperCollins). His collection of Rumi translations was published in 2014 and received a 4.5-star rating on Goodreads. In 2015, Dhondy interviewed his close friend V. S. Naipaul in India and in London as part of the Jaipur Literature Festival and his publishers produced a collection of his works in an anthology.

Contents

Foreword

A final valediction

Geordie Greig

Twenty years ago when I first met Vidia Naipaul he was considered the most intimidating figure in the literary world. He would send journalists packing after two questions if he felt they had not read his works. When I went to interview him at his home in Wiltshire his wife Nadira took pity on me and asked him be kind.

And he was – for the next 20 years. While he had a reputation as irascible and fearsome, and his observations and prose were as sharp as glass, his candour, vulnerability, gentleness and gestures of generosity were equally moving. Towards me that generosity included having two books, including the masterly A Bend in the River, dedicated to me.

His books explored identity and loss, corruption and different kinds of exile. And he was often himself the subject, the poor boy from Trinidad who made his way on a scholarship to Oxford with one goal: to write. And he never felt that it was easy. He talked to me, occasionally in tears, of his struggle and the almost impossible task of making words be more than mere words and letters to create literary masterpieces. At one stage that urge to succeed turned to despair and he attempted to end his life. But then his writing succeeded beyond all expectation as he carved a position as a titan of literature.

His very last night on 11 August 2018, I was called to his bedside as he slipped away. His wife, Nadira, held his hands, just days before his 86th birthday, as he gently breathed his last while I read aloud Tennyson's 'Crossing the Bar', one his favourite poems. It was a peaceful end for a man who masterfully made his mark by disrupting complacency to made truth arresting.

He worked so relentlessly hard, sacrificing all social life in his early days which meant that he was astounded to discover in the last two decades that he also on occasion loved going out. He would jest that Harry's Bar, the high society Mayfair Club to which he was incongruously made an honorary member in his eighties, was the place that made the best dry martini. His first wage at the BBC had been eight guineas a week. But then he always insisted his vision was comic.

He found it impossible not to face difficult truths with candour and courage. He had no time for cant. 'I don't want to read Proust. It is for idlers or people who want to sound educated,' he would say, laughing. And humour, looking askance at the world, was an essential part of him. Yes, he invited controversy as, after Salman Rushdie had a fatwa issued against him in 1989, he wittily described it as 'a severe form of literary criticism'. In some ways, Vidia was like Salim, the hero in *A Bend in the River*, 'a man without side'. He was the observer who changed the way we look at the world.

Like Naipaul, Salim has no illusions, declaring in a celebrated opening line: 'The world is what it is; men who are nothing, who allow themselves to become nothing, have no place in it.'

Note on the contributor

Geordie Greig is editor of the *Daily Mail*. Previously, he was editor of the *Mail on Sunday*.

Introduction

A giant with feet of clay?

John Mair

On 11 August 2018, in London, a literary colossus died: Sir Vidiadhar Surajprasad (V. S.) Naipaul on the eve of his 86th birthday. Colossus he was but was he a giant with feet of clay?

The obituaries/reviews have been mixed to put it mildly. Varying from the hagiographic to the plain hostile. V. S. was a man who made enemies easily. In his life he was garlanded with the Nobel Prize and a British knighthood plus literary awards galore. He basked in the light of that glory. V. S. was seen as a total master of the craft of writing, praise which he enjoyed, but also a 'difficult' (for which read cantankerous) individual.

He used his words as if each was special. Reading him is like listening to a masterful symphony. The canon of work he left behind is huge: sixteen works of fiction and fourteen works of non-fiction in a writing career that spanned nearly six decades. One of his literary heroes was Joseph Conrad and he all but exceeded his literary footprint.

It was in his non-fiction where his controversialist nature came to the fore. He was a 'fireman' writer: if he saw a conflagration or conflict then he headed towards it rather than the other way .No issue was too big or too complicated for him not to engage with and maybe plough a lonely intellectual furrow around or against: The Caribbean past, present and future, the state of Africa and of 'Mother India', Islam worldwide, women and feminism, race.

Many saw V. S. as having become a boring old reactionary in his later years. Was this accurate? His twilight days were, indeed, spent amongst the retired admirals, generals and former Russian spies in the rural Wiltshire countryside of southern England – a long way away from the South Trinidad Chaguanas and Port of Spain of his youth. His life truly was a journey.

This book is not all hagiography. We give full rein to his critics .There is much critique from Professor Orlando Patterson, of Harvard, and Narissa Deokarran, a Guyana-based blogger. The first section explores the theme 'V. S.: the man'. The second section draws together a series of essays on his love/hate relationship with Trinidad. Next comes a section focusing on Naupaul's literary legacy while the fourth takes in some of the many controversies surrounding his views on Islam, women, India and so on. The final section incorporates the tributes – and a few intimate memories – of some of those who knew V. S. personally and had brief encounters with him.

We hope the book reflects well the work of a literary giant and the vibrant debate about his legacy. It could not have come to fruition (so quickly thanks to the miracle of the internet) without the hard work editing of Professor Richard Lance Keeble, the intuition of Farrukh Dhondy and the constant support of Kenneth Ramchand and Kirk Meighoo in Trinidad. Special thanks to our publisher, Paul Davies, and to all our contributors for providing such excellent copy so rapidly.

Enjoy it!

Section 1

V. S.: the man

John Mair

Farrukh Dhondy is V. S. Naipaul's latter-day Boswell – 'that boy' as V. S. labelled his fellow writer. In a brilliant, highly personal, opening essay, he recalls getting through to Naipaul on the day his Nobel Prize for literature was announced. The BBC was after Dhondy for comment.

> I immediately rang Vidia's Wiltshire home. Nadira answered the phone and said the place had gone wild with TV crews and reporters from all over the world invading the neat and quiet village of Salterton.
>
> She said he was being serially interviewed, but he'd interrupt these and come to the phone as she was sure he'd like to speak to me. Vidia came on.
>
> 'Farrukh, Farrukh, you've heard of my little spot of good luck,' he said.
>
> I recall the moment because it was part of Vidia's modesty, an attribute which is strongly evident in his writing and was, to me, in his personality – though to his detractors, calling V. S. Naipaul 'modest' is tantamount to calling Hitler compassionate.

Dhondy is easily the most vocal current cheerleader for V. S.:

He always said that writing if it's worth anything has to provoke. As for his standing amongst other writers, one can say they are as slingless Davids to his Goliath with a plethora of slings, if not literary and observational AK47s. His writing takes many forms, none of them copies of anything that has gone before. Throughout his conversations with me, for formal published interviews or relaxed *gupp-shupp* ('idle talk' --he would have hated the description) between friends, he would extol the fresh and the underivative.

Professor Kenneth Ramchand is more objective. He wrote a masterly obituary in the *Guardian* about his fellow 'Trini' and his use of the English language:

> V. S. Naipaul constructed clear, irreducible sentences, and marshalled them into single-minded paragraphs. His control of language and the rhetoric of his novels were such that he could persuade you into belief even when his truths were only partly true.

One of his sworn enemies who became a firm friend in later life is the distinguished writer Paul Theroux. They had taught together in East Africa, fell out very badly and for three decades had a very public spat. One of the great literary feuds *de nos jours*. It ended at a British literary event as Theroux recalls:

> Ten years passed in silence. At the Hay Festival, I was sitting with Ian McEwan when Naipaul appeared at the door of a big tent, Nadira and her daughter supporting him on each arm as he moved slowly through the gathering, limping, breathing hard.

> 'Say something to him,' Ian said. I said I didn't dare. He said: 'Go on. Life is too short.'

> Provoked, I went up to Vidia and said hello and he took my hand warmly and held on. 'I've missed you,' I said. He said: 'I've missed you, too.'

V. S. delighted and frustrated his fellow Caribbeans in equal measure. Professor Clem Seecharan is one of the great historiographers of the region. Cricket, Jagan, Berbice: his palette is wide. Like Naipaul, he is a Hindu Indo-Caribbean but from Guyana, not Trinidad, and one generation younger. Seecharan enjoyed the loosening of Indo mores which provided both a straightjacket and a lodestar for V. S.

> I did not have to endure or negotiate those Brahminic certainties. I was not marooned ('shipwrecked') in the Brahmin's universe of rituals and ceremonies; neither did I have to endure people in the mass, day after day, under the same roof. I did not have to take preferential treatment or adulation for granted. I could not become complacent: my people had to earn whatever respect seeped their way, so did I. Therefore, in spite of Naipaul's rejection of his Trinidadian Brahmin roots, it planted in him snobbishness, a lack of manners, a hard certainty, superciliousness with regard to his own intellectual powers and an incapacity for magnanimity or gratitude. Maybe all of this is a mask for an underlying cultural insecurity, but the hardness has kept him going. The hardness has sustained the mission. The hardness has enabled this great mind to work single-mindedly, undeterred by its many detractors, over several decades. It has given the way of seeing its pertinacity.

Professor David Dabydeen, a fellow Indo-Guyanese, recalls the horrors of putting V. S. in front of an English university audience. It was a minefield of sensibilities. Despite that experience, he sees beyond the mask to the man and the writer:

> I think he relished being galling, and creating a nasty persona and putting distance between himself and voyeurs (in his mind literary critics, journalists, etc). By all accounts he was a cruel man, but he had greatness in him, and what mattered was the writing, not the person or persona.

Professor Hilary Beckles, Vice-Chancellor of the region's blue riband University of the West Indies (UWI), is warm in his appreciation:

> Our literary genius was quintessentially a West Indian intellectual, struggling with the contradictory consciousness of post-colonialism, including the parodies and pleasures of imperial culture. He was torn and tortured at every turn, and never sought to find solace or inner peace in any conciliatory conceptual discourse. Instead, he dug deeper into the reality he felt could not be repaired. Home, he felt, was filled with pain, and now he will never return to it again.

Finally in this section, the Street Fighting Man turned north London intellectual, Tariq Ali, places V. S. firmly in his historical past:

> He never saw himself as just another face in the mural of 20th-century literature. The mural was, in any case, not his favourite art form. He loved and possessed a very fine collection of Persian and Indian miniatures. But this wasn't a frame in which he saw himself either. Long before the knighthood and the Nobel Prize, it was the mirror that excited him. Destiny stared him in the face every morning. He believed in himself. The Trinidadian was to become a very fine writer of English prose.

Chapter 1

'Farrukh, Farrukh, you've heard of my little spot of good luck'

In this portrait of his friend Vidia Naipaul, Farrukh Dhondy remembers him as the constantly entertaining guru – and how he responded, so modestly, on hearing he had won the Nobel Prize for literature.

With Dylan Thomas one rages against the dying of the light. Sir V. S. Naipaul, Vidia, died six days before his eighty-sixth birthday. He was, in the eyes of friends and most critics, even those whose negative views are represented in this collection, one of the most important writers of the twentieth century. His individual talent forged a tradition rather than coming from one.

There remain unique and distinguishing characteristics of his work and they were painstakingly and even painfully achieved.

He often told me that he conceived the ambition to be a writer very early in his life. The raw ambition didn't involve knowing what to write. He said he 'hadn't discovered his material'.

The Trinidad in which he grew up had no sustained tradition of writing. In his childhood and before, there were those who wrote stories about the Caribbean islands in imitation of European or American story-writers such as O'Henry or Somerset Maugham, stories which had transformed settings but no originality. They had initiated no new ways of seeing.

Vidia seemed grateful rather than despairing that he had no one to follow, no one he respected enough to imitate. For a young man with the ambition to write, that's a fortunate limbo.

And then one day his material found him. Genre writers, who write crime novels or the modern mythologies of Enid Blyton or Harry Potter, don't have to wait for that moment. They can use fragments from material that's gone before and place them in predictable invention. J. K. Rowling had the mythical depiction of public school life from *Tom Brown's Schooldays* and the tradition of magic and myth from C. S. Lewis and Tolkien.

The material that first came to Vidia was the voice of Trinidadian streets which became the concatenation of stories in *Miguel Street* (1959). Several 'Caribbean' novels followed. They drew on the life of his neighbourhood and family in Trinidad, most notably the fictionalised struggles of his father in *A House for Mr. Biswas* (1961).

While these novels gestated and were written, he was commissioned to write a 'travelogue' of the Caribbean which became *The Middle Passage* (1962). Through it, he came upon a method of literary discovery. He would speak to people about their lives and tell their stories, inferring larger 'civilisational' and cultural truths from them.

He says he then left the straitjacket of the Caribbean islands behind physically and creatively. There was, he said, nothing left of any importance to say. Yes, other Caribbean writers have followed him and though they are published and even shortlisted for literary prizes, I can't think of one who can claim to tell the world something different or something more, something the world urgently needs to know, about the displaced cultures of the island societies – descendants of African slaves or Indian indentured labour.

Ruthless determination to describe what he saw

This method of discovery, without any nationalistic baggage or ideological allegiance and with a ruthless determination to describe what he saw or deduce from what he heard, lasted through his career. From *The Middle Passage*, the form of observation and narrative went on to produce *An Area of Darkness* (1964) and subsequent essays and four further books about India – two of them novels in a fresh form. Vidia used the same literary technique in the books about Africa, Argentina and the non-Arab 'Muslim-convert' countries of Iran, Pakistan, Indonesia and Malaysia.

The latter half of the twentieth century was a period of rapid decolonisation and of continents entering new phases of development and, through that, of dramatic turmoil. Again, a case of historic material finding the voice that could explore it and make available its truths.

This certainly involved saying things which those about whom Vidia was saying them wouldn't like. Indians don't want to be told that they defecate without inhibition in the open. They dislike being told that there is a contradictory duality to their thought, which embraces and readily uses the processes and products of modern scientific thinking and still believes that stars, exploding masses of gas in space, form patterns which influence the day to day fortunes of all human lives.

Countries such as Iran don't want to be told that the political ideology they espoused in their support for a republican 'revolution' is a cruel, medieval imposition on a contemporary society. And I have not yet met a Pakistani who does applaud the phrase that Vidia used to describe his-or-her country: 'Pakistan, a criminal enterprise!'

His non-fiction explorations in Africa and the two great novels, *In a Free State* (1971) and *A Bend in the River* (1979), have not won him vast acclaim in the places he writes about. And yet they describe, as no one else dares to, the reality of Africa in painful transition.

Vidia is often compared by academics writing about these African books to Joseph Conrad. To them Conrad's description of 'the horror, the horror' of colonial Africa is acceptable and penetrating because the villain is the coloniser. But when Vidia writes in a similar vein he is accused of 'racism', of being an 'Uncle Tom' and even of 'stereotyping' through his precise descriptions.

Perhaps all those who contribute to the world divide it. I am sure Galileo was not popular with medieval theologians who insisted on believing that the earth was the centre of the universe. Darwin wasn't the darling of those who thought God created all creatures in those six days. Mahatma Gandhi was reviled by Churchill for demanding decolonisation and setting the world on a new political course.

So it was, I think, with Vidia. At a literary conference which I attended, the respected Indian playwright and cultural diplomat, Girish Karnad, in a famous episode which I am compelled to rehearse later, attacked Vidia, calling him an Islamophobe. Elsewhere, fellow Nobel Prize winner Derek Walcott dubbed him 'V. S. Nightfall' and said he was a racist.

In these cases his critics' 'nationalism' overcomes the evidence of their senses. It's as if they adopt a wilful blindness to the degradations of their societies – something that Vidia dedicated himself to describing in all his necessary, revelatory writings.

In his final book about Africa, he describes meeting an African potentate who insisted that, through some primitive magical power, he happened to be present in France and at a dinner table in Ghana at the same time. Vidia's pointing out the absurdity of this nonsense earned him a reiteration of the 'racist' slur. So did his observation that in some Caribbean islands, notably Haiti, there existed more poverty, crime and corruption per square mile than there possibly was evident in Hades.

Corrective stance on Indian history

One of the great political controversies that Vidia's writing stimulated was his corrective stance on Indian history. At the time he wrote *India: A Million Mutinies Now* (1990), his third book on the country, a significant political change was overtaking it.

The end of the last century and the beginning of this one saw the birth and rise to power of the Hindutva parties and factions. The Rashtriya Swayamsevak Sangh, some of whose leaders and members were implicated in the assassination of Mahatma Gandhi, formed a significant ideological block in the newly formed Bharatiya Janata Party (BJP). The leaders of this party overtly embraced a form of nationalism that characterised India as the motherland of Hindus, a declaration of hostility to the millions of Indian Muslims, Christians, Sikhs, Buddhists, Jains, Parsis and even the tribal animists. They engaged in overt attacks on the 'secular' policies and practice of the Congress government which had ruled India since Independence and professed and followed the inclusive stance of Gandhi and Nehru which assiduously supported the separation of religion from politics.

The political movement for Independence, to a significant extent led by them, sought to unite all the religions against the colonial power. The historians who supported this noble stance didn't see it as a strategically essential political doctrine. They adopted the secular ideal as a historical perspective. In his first book about India, Vidia acknowledged and wrote positively about this stance.

In his later books, having explored India at greater length, Naipaul expressed his contempt for what he saw as a concealment, or at best soft-pedalling, of historical truth. He interpreted the Muslim conquest of India, which began in the seventh and eighth centuries and continued through Muslim Sultanate and Mughal dynastic rule to the eighteenth century, as a cruel and even genocidal wiping out of an ancient civilisation.

Vidia characterised the acts of the Muslim rulers as the wiping out of an earlier dominantly Hindu and before it Buddhist culture. He based his contentions on textual evidence from the past – that of travellers and Muslim historians themselves.

The secular strain of opinion which does (and should!) dominate liberal, democratic thought in India caused some of its adherents to see Vidia's attempt to look at the historical past without the Gandhi-Nehru strictures as an assault on Muslims and support for the Hindutva brigade, even so far as accusing him of excusing or being in favour of the Gujarat riots in which thousands of urban Muslims were slaughtered.

Girish Karnad, to whose attack I alluded earlier, with the best of motives, in a famous speech at the Mumbai Literature Live festival, on 31 October 2017, characterised Vidia as a supporter of an ideological and even physical assault on the Muslim population of India. He provided a packed audience with his contentions and the evidence for this prosecution. It may have convinced some, but knowing Vidia I knew it was far from the truth. Vidia wasn't antagonistic to any theological formation. (He may have found certain practices of, say, Christians symbolically worshipping an instrument of capital punishment distasteful. It would, if the messiah were condemned to death today, be like using the electric chair as a symbol of salvation.) Vidia never, in writing or verbally, attacked any theology or any prophet. As far as I could tell, he had a respect for Hindu ritual, was curious about its eschatology but wouldn't call himself a Hindu.

He wasn't anti-Islamic or anti-Muslim. He married a Pakistani Muslim and though I've not seen Nadira, Lady Naipaul, saying her prayers or going to the mosque, she certainly objects to any blasphemous references to the Prophet. Vidia formally adopted her two Muslim children and was grandfather to their offspring. Vidia never thought that drawing back the carpet under which the suppressive, cruel or even genocidal acts of Muslim Indian history has been swept, was tantamount to support for the destructive ideology of Hindu bigotry.

When Vidia met the BJP culturalists

On one trip to India I went to see him at a hotel in Delhi. This was in 1992, soon after the Hindutva brigade had attempted the demolition of the Babri Masjid, the mosque built by the first Mughal Emperor Babur on, the Hindutvatis claim, the sacred site of an ancient Hindu temple.

'When do you return, Farrukh?' he asks.

'Tomorrow morning.'

'Can you stay for a day longer? I want you to come with us to a meeting to which I'm invited of the BJP's Cultural Wing.'

'Isn't that an oxymoron?' I say.

'Now, now. Don't be clever, Farrukh,' says Vidia.

I stay the extra day and we go and are greeted by some stalwarts of the party. The TV crews and journalists are at the gate and being held back by security as we drive in and alight.

Vidia tells the assembled crowd in the hall, the BJPs culturalists, that he is there to ask them questions and to listen and not to make a speech. He asks them why and in what way they are revising history books. I sit in the corner seat of the front row in the audience as the witness that Vidia wanted, as he is convinced that there will be those who will distort and twist anything he says and even make it up.

There are answers from the floor to his several queries, some of which talk about 'correcting' school history books and some of which are vituperative rubbish.

Then someone makes bold to ask Vidia about the Babri Masjid and whether he supports the action that the volunteer marchers have taken in attempting its demolition. Vidia says he is only certain that the Mughal conqueror Babur built the mosque as an act of hubris. I found myself wondering how many in that audience understood the word.

As we emerged from the hall the press and cameras had forced themselves through the gate and besieged us. The questions began to fly.

'Naipaul, do you condone the slaughter of Muslims in Gujarat?'

Vidia posed as though he was about to answer. Nadira was shouting back, fielding the antagonistic questions which were framed like the classical 'have you stopped beating your wife?'

I grabbed Vidia's arm. 'Let's go, they are trying to set you up.'

'I want to be set up,' he said.

I dragged him away and we escaped the apparent hostility.

Sure enough, Vidia's expectation and precaution in asking me to accompany them proved right. Two well-known writers wrote critical and even accusatory articles in the Indian-English press implying that they were reporting on the meeting as though they were present at it. They weren't.

The animus against Vidia, the accusations of racism, Islamophobia, misogyny and Allah-knows-what, are sometimes justified reactions to his opinionated pronouncements, but very often reactions of the wounded to the keenly observed, precisely pronounced and possibly hurtful truth.

Vidia's legacy is the arrogant observation of the realities of our world in all its transitions and the examination in his fictional works of characters in worlds of historical flux.

Window-pane prose: we look through it at the object beyond

His prose, fictional and non-fictional, the prose of discovery, has been called window-pane prose. We look through it at the object beyond, unlike the meretricious, stained-glass prose of some writers, which vainly calls attention to itself and its conceits.

Derek Walcott's assertion, supported by many writers and given space in no less than the *New York Review of Books*, that Vidia's critical insights in his writing amount to racism are based on personal animus. In his book *A Writer's People* (2007), Vidia writes about coming upon Walcott's early poems and being fascinated by the very fact that they existed; that a Caribbean poet had made a distinctive contribution to letters.

In this chapter on Walcott, Vidia traces the progression of his view of literature as he confronts the world of writing. He sees and provides insights into the limitations imposed on writers by the worlds they come from or the ones they embrace. It leads him to analyse the scope and limitations of West Indian writers whose work he characterises, sometimes negatively. Walcott was obviously not pleased.

In the same book, Vidia does not hesitate to apply the similarly severe, if broader, strictures to British writers and to his sometime friend Anthony Powell. The book is in no sense colour-conscious and in itself provides no evidence for calling Vidia a racist.

Those who criticise Vidia's books about Africa, the Caribbean and the countries which converted to Islam, inevitably accuse him of 'having a colonial attitude and eye'. That's merely an idle form of abuse. Vidia's distinction and uniqueness as a writer is to address the countries and continents he explores and describes through the lives and discourse of people he encounters in the first half-century after the collapse of colonialism.

His famous novel, *A Bend in the River*, begins: 'The world is what it is...' and Vidia wanted to see it exactly as it was without any fog of ideology, lens of nationalism, distorting mirror of received opinion or filter of political correctness. Abandoning those mediating instruments, he offered himself as a target for ideologues, for the unbalanced nationalists of India, the Caribbean or Africa, for the defenders of the regimes of Iran and Pakistan, for readers and followers of clichéd opinion and for the politically-correct wallahs.

He always said that writing if it's worth anything has to provoke. As for his standing amongst other writers, one can say they are as slingless Davids to his Goliath with a plethora of slings, if not literary and observational AK47s. His writing takes many forms, none of them copies of anything that has gone before. Throughout his conversations with me, for formal published interviews or relaxed *gupp-shupp* ('idle talk' --he would have hated the description) between friends, he would extol the fresh and the underivative.

He once read me a passage from *Pickwick Papers* and said nobody had looked at that small segment of the world in that way. He thought it was wonderful. He then picked up *A Tale of Two Cities* and read a paragraph or two of description from it, remarking that it was inexact, clichéd and derived from Dickens's earlier books. I pointed out that *Tale* was the only book written at a historical distance from Dickens's own life. Vidia said it was not seen but imagined.

His own quest in writing was to turn the imagined into the seen.

One contention that may commentators on his career and personality have written about, including Paul Theroux – who went from being a friend to one of his severest critics and then resumed his friendship and presumably recanted – is that V. S. Naipaul was a great writer and an awful person. Some of this opinion doesn't rely on any personal experience but draws on Patrick French's biography for derogatory 'facts' about Vidia's life.

I happened to be present on occasions when Patrick was recording Vidia's testimony about his past when he initiated talk about things which he had done of which he was not proud. I asked him later why he was putting these, some detrimental confessions, in the public domain and he said the truth was what it was and one must have it represented, dirty linen and all. I feel compelled to say that not all the nasty 'facts' in Patrick's biography were volunteered by Vidia --- some of the seedier ones, which Vidia vehemently denied, were supplied by people who felt they had been wronged by him.

Vidia refused to read any reviews of his work or news about him though I was determined to slip these into our conversations. I once told him that someone had written a piece extolling his 'prose style'. Unusually for him, Vidia seized on the comment and said he didn't understand why people carried on about his 'style'. He said he didn't think he had any. He attempted to use the simplest words to make the physical or the abstract come to the reader in glaring and clear focus. Style indeed.

Vidia didn't tolerate fools (defined quite widely) gladly

A thorough critical assessment of Vidia's work is not in the scope of this essay, which is written in the wake of our loss. I want to write about my friend, inspiration and constantly engaging guru and even entertainer, Vidia, 'the boss' – and 'mamaji' when he was out of earshot.

It's true that Vidia didn't tolerate fools gladly. The definition of 'fools' was for him quite wide and he made his dissension from their opinions or points of view quite evident. I might occasionally have fitted into one of these definitions, but he gave no sign of not tolerating me.

I first came across V. S. Naipaul as a name in the serendipitously named magazine *Encounter*. It was unlike the other names in so far as it wasn't European and though I was an avid reader of Indian writers and writers on

India at the time, I didn't think that they could penetrate the glass ceiling of international literary publications. It was a landmark.

Then came *An Area of Darkness*, his first book on India. Years later he told me that it was the product of disillusion. He came to India to acquaint himself with the country of his forefathers and though he was brought up with its religious myths and its nationalist fervour his writer's mind was a clean slate. There's a sense of shock in the book. Observation trumps ideological or nationalist bias. If Indians defecated in the streets and in many places where he looked, he would say so. If a prominent Indian scientist who could make a nuclear bomb using advanced modern physics believed he could also get his daughter married through the pronouncements of her horoscope, he would point out the intellectually schizoid nature of some Indian thinking. If he was the guest of some rich Indian family who gathered pretentious imitation-Picasso pictures and hung them in their drawing rooms with conceits of being connoisseurs of art, he would ridicule them. It wasn't surprising then that critics of the book called it, in line with other critical, perhaps politically motivated books such as Katherine Mayo's *Mother India* (1927), 'the gutter inspector's report'.

I read it while I was in college in Pune, intrigued by the accuracy and the obdurate insistence on honest observation and comment. I didn't tell my determinedly nationalist or patriotic friends that this gutter was absolutely necessary to inspect and perhaps pour some literary disinfectant on. I read it in cowardly, silent agreement.

I met V. S. on a few occasions in London but my first real encounter with him was when the BBC asked me to review his third (or fourth, if you count shorter essays) book, *India: A Million Mutinies Now* and interview him. We talked about the possible territory we'd cover and then went on camera. I observed that the judgements in this last book were discernably more positive than those in the first two or three books.

'Oh dear, you're giving me marks already!' he said.

All I could do was to attempt a justification of 'giving him marks' by quoting from the books and asking him to agree that a certain progress was evident. There was in *Mutinies* a determination to find seeds of positive social growth through the personal stories of the people he interrogated.

I don't think he liked that interview and when I asked him to sign the first editions of his books which I had hopefully brought along, he said he'd sign just one. Having done that, he left the interview room and walked down the pavements to his flat in South Kensington. No small talk.

Years later, Nadira and Nancy Sladek, the editor of the *Literary Review*, showed Vidia that interview which Nancy had recorded, pointing out to him that the interviewer (me) was falling over himself to be positive and meeting with a sullen response. That interview was a year or so before I got a call in my office – I was earning my living as a TV bureaucrat at the time – from Gillon Aitken, Vidia's agent, who said Vidia wanted to have lunch with me. I was somewhat surprised and said I didn't think he liked me.

'That's all changed,' Gillon said. 'You know he's married Nadira and she is a great fan of your books and your columns in *Asian Age* which she diligently reads and has persuaded him to invite you to lunch.'

The beginning of a deep friendship

The lunch took place and I noticed that while Nadira was very amiable, Vidia remained sullen until I was asked what my latest TV offering on Channel Four would be. I said I had just returned from Jamaica where my TV crew had recorded the proceedings in a hospital in Kingston. My story was that one day I and the crew encountered a tall security guard at the gates, who detained us saying we had to record him singing as he was 'the Nat King Cole of Jamaica'.

Vidia, at last, looked curious.

I said I had asked the cameraman to switch on and record Jamaica's King Cole who began to sing 'Mona Lisa, Mona Lisa...'etc. He was thirty seconds into the song when loud gunshots rang out from somewhere nearby. We were inclined to duck for cover when Nat said: 'Don't mind dem boys, don't mind dem!' and kept singing even louder to drown the gunshots. We ran into the hospital. Soon the wounded and the dead from that encounter followed us.

I said I wanted to start the series about the Jamaican hospital with whatever we had on camera of that scene. Vidia laughed – and laughed. It was probably Jamaica as he knew it.

It was the beginning of a deep friendship.

When the Swedish Academy announced that they were giving the Nobel Prize for literature to Vidia, I happened to be in India. The BBC rang me and the BBC researcher, at the end of my mobile phone, asked if I had a land-line. I asked what this was about and she said she wanted to speak to me about my friend V. S. Naipaul. The first thought that occurred was that he was dead.

'What? Why?' I asked and she calmly said because he'd won the Nobel Prize. Phew!

She booked me for the programme and I immediately rang Vidia's Wiltshire home. Nadira answered the phone and said the place had gone wild with TV crews and reporters from all over the world invading the neat and quiet village of Salterton.

She said he was being serially interviewed, but he'd interrupt these and come to the phone as she was sure he'd like to speak to me. Vidia came on.

'Farrukh, Farrukh, you've heard of my little spot of good luck,' he said.

I recall the moment because it was part of Vidia's modesty, an attribute which is strongly evident in his writing and was, to me, in his personality – though to his detractors, calling V. S. Naipaul 'modest' is tantamount to calling Hitler compassionate.

Note on the contributor

Farrukh Dhondy is an Indian-born British writer, playwright, screenwriter and left-wing activist of Parsi descent who resides in the United Kingdom. He is well-known not only for his writing but also for his film and TV work.

Chapter 2

The futility of human effort – the key Naipaulian preoccupation

The greatest literary virtue of V. S. Naipaul was instant readability, according to Kenneth Ramchand.

V. S. Naipaul constructed clear, irreducible sentences, and marshalled them into single-minded paragraphs. His control of language and the rhetoric of his novels were such that he could persuade you into belief even when his truths were only partly true.

Naipaul, the winner of the 2001 Nobel Prize for literature, was regarded by many as the greatest novelist of his time. In his early fictions he trusted description, character, dialogue and event to evoke the world that had shaped him. Beneath the comedy and the almost kindly satire of these early works there are glimpses of the bleak view of human existence and effort and self-fictionalising that were to become the key themes and motifs of his later work.

The first of his 14 non-fiction works, *The Middle Passage* (1962), was a lively if unsparing report on West Indian societies as 'half-made societies that seemed doomed to remain half-made' because they lacked the self-knowledge or the will to reinvent themselves in the independence period. By 1970, the urge to express ideas and opinions about a world growing everywhere more unstable and insecure began to take hold.

He admired journalism (the occupation of his father, Seepersad Naipaul) because it was much better than the novel at keeping up realistically with the changing world. To widen his net he started to shape combinations (*In a Free State*, 1971), hybrids (*The Enigma of Arrival*, 1987), and 'sequences'

(*A Way in the World*, 1994) that blurred distinctions between fiction and non-fiction.

The Middle Passage (tame in hindsight) was followed by frequent travel and more on-the-spot coverage of peoples and countries in turmoil. The liberties he was to take with language registers and genres, and his ability to evoke different settings, are displayed with aplomb in *In a Free State*, a pageant of placelessness and insecurity that won him the Booker Prize in 1971.

Of his 29 books, at least seven are likely to endure: his first collection of stories, *Miguel Street* (1959); the three novels *A House for Mr. Biswas* (1961), *The Mimic Men* (1967) and *A Bend in the River* (1979); a work of non-fiction, *The Loss of El Dorado* (1969), an original and challenging historical work on the making of Trinidad and its polyglot capital, Port of Spain, that Naipaul described as 'the synthesis of the worlds and cultures that had made me'; the global fiction *In a Free State* (1971); and the ambitious *The Enigma of Arrival* (1987), part autobiography, part fiction, part meditation on life, time, death and the writing life.

Realistically rendered detail of his enduring works

In these works, he created palpable geographical, social and cultural contexts in which to locate people, their stories and their emotions; and in all of them, symbolism and ideas of universal import spring unforced out of realistically rendered detail.

The scholarship in *The Loss of El Dorado* added conviction to the key Naipaulian preoccupation with the futility of human effort and the perils of the impossible dream. Much of his experience as a student at Oxford and as an anxious inhabitant of London in the 1950s was filtered into the constitution of Ralph Singh, the narrating character of *The Mimic Men*. In this novel, the miscellaneous collection of misfits and refugees with whom Singh associates for a time were soon to become a conscious part of Naipaul's vision of a restless world of people cut off from the landscapes of their birth and not able to find purchase somewhere else. He was the first writer to stumble upon this theme and he took it further than anybody else.

His native island, the former British colony of Trinidad, with its extraordinary meeting of peoples and cultures, was his seedbed. Long after he decided he would never live in Trinidad and Tobago, he could still say: 'From the writing point of view, this land is pure gold ... pure, pure gold.'

Trinidad made and haunted the writer, and the evidence is in many of his books.

Born in Chaguanas, on Trinidad's west coast, south of Port of Spain, Vidia was the second of the seven children of Seepersad and his wife, Droapatie (née Capildeo). They were married in 1929, the year that Seepersad began his journalistic career as the Chaguanas correspondent of the *Trinidad Guardian*. Vidia's early childhood was mostly spent in or near the Capildeo family residence known as the Lion House, a unique example of North Indian architecture that dominated the main street of Chaguanas, a country town in the sugar belt where the majority of Trinidad Indians lived. Seepersad quickly felt his individuality threatened by the communal life of the Capildeos. The acute tensions of this period would have been felt by his son.

Stories both comic and compassionate

When the chance came in 1938 to work in Port of Spain, as a full-time reporter with the *Trinidad Guardian*, Seepersad left Chaguanas to occupy rooms in a Capildeo house in Luis Street, in the Woodbrook district. The move in 1938 introduced the six-year-old Vidia to the life of the street, the pleasures and sights of the city and, in due course, to the cinema, all of which were to inform the comic and compassionate stories and sketches of *Miguel Street*.

From 1938 to 1942, Vidia was a pupil at Tranquillity Boys' School, after which he began his 'sound colonial education' at Queen's Royal College (QRC), the country's oldest and most British secondary school. At the same time, he witnessed his father working at being a writer, self-publishing in 1943 a remarkable collection of stories, *Gurudeva and Other Indian Tales*. 'I loved them as writing, as well as for the labour I had seen going into their making.'

Seepersad's example made it possible for a young boy in a colony to dream of a literary career. The purchase of a house of his own in 1946 brought much-needed relief to Seepersad. To Vidia, in his last two years at QRC, and to the family, it brought peace and desperately needed stability.

In 1950, Naipaul went to University College, Oxford, to study English and become a writer. Five years later, he married Patricia Hale, who would be the one reliable element in his life for 41 years until her death. Pat may not have been his muse but she remained in all seasons note-taker, sounding board, listener to drafts, common reader and excited fan.

A stillborn first novel as well as book-reviewing for the *New Statesman* would have made it clear enough that Naipaul did not really want to be (could not be) the kind of writer envisaged by the raw 18-year-old in *The Enigma of Arrival*. The example of Seepersad's book and the older man's constant recommendation of West Indian raw material were reinforced by the years Naipaul spent as editor of the BBC'S *Caribbean Voices* programme, reading hundreds of manuscripts from the islands and sharing fellowship with the writers hanging out in the freelances' room at the BBC.

When he started to turn to his natural raw material, it was to three of those writers, the Caribbean Andrew Salkey and Gordon Woolford and an Englishman, John Stockbridge, that he excitedly ran with what became the opening story of *Miguel Street*: 'Without that fellowship, without the response of the three men who read the story, I might not have wanted to go on.' After the breakthrough, he produced *The Mystic Masseur* (1957) and *The Suffrage of Elvira* (1958) in quick time and then tussled with his demons for three years to land his greatest work, *A House for Mr. Biswas*.

In London in 1958, in a time of different stresses, he was able to go back in memory to the traumas of life in the Lion House and to the years in Woodbrook as raw material for his masterpiece. The three-generational novel depicts the exposure of descendants of Indians to the shifting society of Trinidad and describes their evolution from 1906 to 1953. Comic richness arises from the battles between Mr. Biswas and his in-laws, and the manic journalism of the main character who, like his prototype, Seepersad Naipaul, works on the city newspaper. Mr. Biswas saw that the world is what it is and refused to allow himself to be nothing.

Innovations in the genre of travel writing

Naipaul was well regarded for the innovations in the genre of travel writing, and spoke of valuing them above his novels, an opinion that few readers would endorse. He travelled to the Americas, Africa, India, Mauritius, Indonesia, Iran, Pakistan and every corner of the earth touched by invader or coloniser to report on failed and failing states and to expose what he regarded as the malformed or undeveloped selves in them. He stocked his 'travel' books with character, scene and dialogue and rendered episodes.

He wanted *Beyond Belief: Islamic Excursions among the Converted Peoples* (1998) to be thought of as a book of people and stories unshaped by the writer's opinions, but opinion and idea dominated his later work. His topics included imperialism, freedom, emergent nationalisms, religion, revolution, fundamentalism and the colonial mentality. He saw the terror waiting to be unleashed upon the world by half-baked revolutions, mutinies and holy wars, and by fundamentalism and fanaticism of any kind. By the 1990s he had made himself the cynical poet of post-imperialism and the peculiar prophet of violence, global disorientation and homelessness. He was considered by many to be the first modern global writer.

His fellow West Indians began having difficulties with Naipaul early in his career. He was accused of writing 'castrated satire'. A sentence in *The Middle Passage* that 'history is built around achievement and creation; and nothing was ever created in the West Indies' has been held unforgivingly as proof that he was anti-West Indian. He has been accused of racial prejudice against people of African origin, for saying that Africa has no future, and for presenting women negatively.

In 2008, he gave fuel to his critics by allowing an authorised biography, *The World Is What It Is*, by Patrick French, to publicise bold confessions about his visits to prostitutes, intimate details of his obnoxious behaviour towards Pat and his mistress, Margaret Gooding, and many of the cruelties attending his relationships with them and other people. He acted as if he did not care. He would sacrifice anyone or anything for his vocation.

He saw himself as a man without a place. With *The Middle Passage*, Naipaul had effectively written off Trinidad and the West Indies as places to live. After writing *An Area of Darkness* (1964), he knew that whatever it might mean to him, India was not home. Within months of the publication of *The Mimic Men*, the life he had been constructing for himself as a literary figure in the UK was shaken by Britain's new immigration laws.

He flirted briefly with the idea of living in Trinidad. In July 1968 he and his wife were settling in Canada, but by September had changed their minds and returned to the UK. It was at this time that Naipaul completed *In a Free State*, an overwhelming map of dislocation, of fractured worlds, and of damaged individuals in a violent free state. At the end of 1970, Naipaul's friends rescued him from his own dislocation. A bungalow on the grounds of Wilsford Manor in Wiltshire was secured for him at a minimal rent, and after 11 years as tenants there, the Naipauls moved into their own house, Dairy Cottage.

Later life dominated by triangular relationship

His life from 1972 to 1995 was dominated by a triangular relationship with Pat, who stayed at home, and Gooding, an Argentinian woman whom Naipaul met in Buenos Aires in 1972. Their tempestuous affair was conducted in several continents for more than 20 years, and was terminated abruptly by Naipaul only in 1995, when Pat was dying of cancer and he met and proposed to Nadira Khannum Alvi in Pakistan. He received in this period almost every major literary award and recognition, including a knighthood in 1990. He established himself as a phenomenon and a spectacle, 'the writer' personified.

His outstanding work of this period was *A Bend in the River* (1979), a real novel issuing from a novelist possessed. It is Naipaul's most frightening presentation of a world without meaning or the possibility of meaning. Meaninglessness and ineffectuality became his subject in *Half a Life* (2001) and *Magic Seeds* (2004), which pick dispassionately through the unremarkable life of Willie Chandran, from India to London to Africa to India, and back again to London, making an epic of nonentity and purposelessness. Naipaul secretes into them elements from earlier books and his own life in London as if to remind us how fragile are the foundations, and against what dispiriting odds anything is achieved in the world.

His meaning for the island of his birth, and for the world after centuries of empires and colonies, 'everything of value' as he put it in his Nobel lecture, was in his books: 'I am the sum of my books.' In time, that will be seen as his most appropriate epitaph.

In 1996, he married Nadira. She survives him, along with their daughter, Maleeha, and his sisters Mira, Savi and Nalini.

Note on the contributor

Kenneth Ramchand is a graduate of Edinburgh University where he began his career as Lecturer in English. He served for ten years as an Independent Senator in the government of Trinidad and Tobago. He is Professor Emeritus of West Indian Literature, University of the West Indies, and Professor Emeritus of English, Colgate University, NY. He also served as

President of the University of Trinidad and Tobago where, as Associate Provost, he established that university's Academy for Arts, Letters, Culture and Public Affairs. This obituary (slightly amended here) first appeared in the *Guardian* at https://www.theguardian.com/books/2018/aug/12/vs-naipaul-obituary

Chapter 3

Vidia – and the lonely child amidst all the bustle of busy roads

Paul Theroux, author of *Sir Vidia's Shadow*, remembers times spent with Naipaul after reconnecting with him at the Hay Festival.

I visited Vidia Naipaul in his hospital room in London. This was in June. He strained to speak, but we managed to hold a conversation, and he smiled when I reminded him of trips we'd taken together in East Africa, more than fifty years ago.

His belief, his severity in reading my work ('I warn you, I'm brutal'), his pride in his own work – he truly believed in his gift – helped make me a writer. When my work succeeded, he was proud of me, but he felt that he was poorly represented, that his publisher took him for granted, that in spite of his many prizes and honours his readership was small. With a new agent and different publishers, his fortunes improved. But, with more people listening, he became ever more a provocateur, claiming that women can't write, that James Joyce is overrated, or that Princess Anne's daughter had 'a criminal face'. In all the obituaries that have been written, there are many instances of these – Vidia's tantrums and provocations, his outrageous, mood-driven frustrations.

Vidia was at last happy at home and still productive. The upshot of our estrangement was that I had a fabulous subject: my thirty-year friendship with him, which I recounted in *Sir Vidia's Shadow*. It seemed to me a great opportunity, because so many books chronicle love affairs, but how many are about friendship, that purer connection, especially one that goes sour?

Ten years passed in silence. At the Hay Festival, I was sitting with Ian McEwan when Naipaul appeared at the door of a big tent, Nadira and her daughter supporting him on each arm as he moved slowly through the gathering, limping, breathing hard.

'Say something to him,' Ian said. I said I didn't dare. He said: 'Go on. Life is too short.'

Provoked, I went up to Vidia and said hello and he took my hand warmly and held on. 'I've missed you,' I said. He said: 'I've missed you, too.'

'One of the happiest moments of my life'

This instance of forgiveness (because my book had been unsparing) is one of the happiest moments of my life. So we reconnected, exchanged letters and phone calls. We met in India and in New York, and, to my great pleasure, Nadira formed a friendship with my wife, Sheila. More than a friendship – they describe themselves as sisters.

A happy ending, for two writers whose work seldom dramatised happy endings.

I especially loved being in India with him, because it was his obsessive subject. But, one day, a strange thing happened. We were being driven to Amber Fort, outside of Jaipur. Vidia looked out the side window as the car was delayed in traffic at a crowded intersection. A small boy, no more than four or five, was seated on a triangular section of broken pavement between two busy roads. The boy was neatly dressed, in a shirt and shorts, cross-legged on a folded square of cloth, at risk amid the confusion of traffic and pedestrians, sadhus, beggars, hawkers with baskets on their head, schoolchildren, bus fumes, pushcarts, motorbikes, and honking horns. The child was animated by the bustle, yet he was alone – no adult near him, no one attending to him.

Naipaul stared sadly at this odd and overlooked boy, and studied the scene for a long moment. As our car began to move on, he said to me: 'I see myself in that child.'

Note on the contributor

Paul Theroux has written many works of fiction and travel writing, including the modern classics *The Great Railway Bazaar*, *The Old Patagonian Express*, *My Secret History*, and *The Mosquito Coast*. He divides his time between Cape Cod and the Hawaiian islands. This chapter is taken from an article which first appeared at https://www.newyorker.com/culture/personal-history/memories-of-v-s-naipaul.

Chapter 4

In Sir Vidia's shadow: out of historical darkness

Clem Seecharan examines how V. S. Naipaul's narrow Brahmin boyhood shaped both the man and his writings.

I come from a people who were immemorially poor, immemorially without a voice.

— V. S. Naipaul, *The Sunday Times*, 16 September 1990.

Away from this world of my grandmother's house ... there was the great unknown – in this island of only 400,000 people. ... As a child I knew almost nothing, nothing beyond what I had picked up in my grandmother's house.

— V. S. Naipaul, 'Two Worlds', Nobel Lecture, 7 December 2001.

To write was to learn.

— V. S. Naipaul, *Finding the Centre* (1984).

In an interview in 2002, Nobel laureate Sir Vidia Naipaul (1932-2018) rejected what he deemed mimicry in contemporary Indian historiography. This, I believe, was aimed at the 'subaltern school'. Naipaul rarely names what he despises; he never acknowledges those for whom he has little respect. He observed:

There is this great sense in India of needing to catch up with what is being done in the world outside. Now they are trying to write this kind of academic history, to keep up with the jargon. There's no human interest, no interest in the people, only interest in the movement – a most abstract interest.[1]

One ignores the great man at one's peril, even when he is at the peak of his arrogance because, ineluctably, a kernel of truth, an uncomfortably illuminating shaft, permeates his most seemingly trite, provocative assertions. I think what repels Naipaul most is the desiccation of learning by the pressure in academia to conform to the reigning theoretical fad. He is revolted by a sort of tyranny of theory in literary and historical studies and the loss of clarity of exposition.

In Naipaul's later travel writings, on India, the American South and the 'converted' peoples in the Islamic world, the diverse narratives of the people he interviews speak for themselves. The character of the societies and their animating impulses are suggested by the verbatim or reported testimonies of his informants (page after page); but the old certainties of judgement do not obtrude. As he explained in 1990, being interviewed by Andrew Robinson after the publication of *India: A Million Mutinies Now*: '... I thought it was better to let India be defined by the experience of the people, rather than writing one's personal reaction to one's feeling about being an Indian and going back.'[2] The generalising impulse gives way to 'a million mutinies': what is knowable is necessarily limited by the complexity and diversity of the human condition. Naipaul has no time for social scientists, even academic historians.

Beyond the theoretical vapourings of academic historians

Naipaul holds arts courses responsible for the decline of the mind: thought clogged by jargon; language despoiled. The basis of his rejection of contemporary historians in India, therefore, seems to be that while claiming to confer agency in history to marginalised men and women, their obsession with academic credibility in the West has driven them into a theoretical quagmire. The so-called subaltern – mired in jargon – is no less submerged. Jargon 'turns living issues into abstractions ... jargon ends by competing with jargon...'[3] He feels that his own attempt at writing history, his book of 1969, *The Loss of El Dorado*, goes beyond the theoretical vapourings of these academic historians. He is not enamoured of their 'overly abstract way of dealing with history'. He explains: '[F]or the two years I lived among the documents, I sought to reconstruct the human story as best I could.' But he does not eschew an 'overarching approach', the possibility of discovering what J. H. Plumb found in *The Loss of El Dorado*, 'truths about society that are ... profound and moving'.[4] The problem, though, is how does Naipaul integrate the 'human' approach – the verbatim narratives of his informants – and the 'overarching' approach with the necessity to generalise (even theorise)? How does he prevent his 'million mutinies' (the testimonies that he sedulously presents), from hanging in the air: valid narratives, arrived at through much toil and skilfully arranged that could exhaust you with their particularity? How does he find the centre?

What are the 'racial' commonalities and intellectual promptings that link me with Naipaul? We are both descendants of Indian indentured labourers from eastern Uttar Pradesh, taken to sugar plantations in the Caribbean in the late 19th century. Naipaul's people went to Trinidad in the 1880s, mine to Demerara (British Guiana) from the 1870s. They were Brahmins; mine Ahirs (contemporary Yadavs), the traditional cattle-herders of Uttar Pradesh and Bihar. His people, though poor, would have made the journey certain of their high place in the Hindu social order; mine did so in despair that their agricultural skills counted for nothing because of chronic land-hunger and caste prejudice in eastern Uttar Pradesh. My people were no less ambitious than his, abstemious in their zeal to own land in British Guiana; jealous, too, of other people's achievements. This was a harsh, highly competitive environment: invidious comparisons were rife yet a spur to effort. For the first time, they could use their skills, as cultivators and cattle-rearers, in a relatively free, achievement-oriented society. They had escaped to an area of possibilities. They sought wealth no less passionately than they practised Hinduism; the discovery that they could achieve so much made them open up, made them less inward looking, more flexible. They became adept at exploiting every niche conducive to gain.

Vidia Naipaul was born in 1932, the same year as my late mother; the sanctions on him, a Brahmin, the custodian of Hindu tradition, would have been unremitting, even if he were 'born an unbeliever'. Brahmins were superior but they did not have the freedom, the easy access to excess of the lower castes. This fused them into certain attitudes in the Caribbean. Their superiority complex transmuted the fear of contamination by dark, lower-caste people onto black people, Africans. In the Brahmin's universe, the latter were relegated beyond the pale, to the subordinate space formerly reserved for Chamars, Doms, Dusads, Dhobis and Bhangis, the outcastes in North Indian villages. Colonial society's own obeisance to light skin reinforced this Indian obsession. Although most Indians in the Caribbean tended to be darker than their Brahmin compatriots, the Indian's partiality for light skin did not diminish. The Brahmin's fear of pollution by the 'Negro' became universal, a reflex among most Indians, including Muslims and converts to Christianity. Even the broader vision engendered by a liberal education could not lessen this corroding impulse. Nothing could shift it, not even Cheddi Jagan's Marxist endeavour of nearly fifty years, his construction of the Guyanese condition, in a countervailing idiom, in terms of class and the class struggle, against local and foreign capital.

Growing up in a void with regard to Indian ancestors

I am of the generation after Naipaul. I was not subject to the social constraints required of the Brahmin. I did not grow up in an extended family, a large group of kin occupying a shared space – in Naipaul's evocative assessment, an enclosing self-sufficient world absorbed with its quarrels and jealousies, as difficult for the outsider to penetrate as for one of its members to escape. It protected and imprisoned...'[5] But both of us grew up in a void with regard to our Indian antecedents, and a longing to look back, heightened by the presence, everywhere, of former 'bound coolies' from India.

Where Naipaul and I depart is in our way of seeing. His was shaped by the narrow Brahmin boyhood. In spite of the precision of the writing, the magnificent gift for detail, the intellectual sagacity that makes him so prescient even when he is cynical – Naipaul lacks empathy. That is why, although he denounces historians in India for aping theoretical fads, for having 'no human interest, no interest in the people', he cannot really reach the cultural and religious promptings at the heart of human endeavour. Naipaul's Brahmin boyhood turned him away from religion, rituals, festivals, the spirit of place, the capacity for trust and friendship. It fused him into a way of seeing that is clinical in its perspicacity, but fundamentally mean in spirit. The revulsion against his own boyhood: the surfeit of Brahminic certainties; the emasculation of his own father, 'imprisoned' in his mother-in-law's compound (the worst possible fate for the male Hindu); the sheer ubiquity and claustrophobia of the huge joint family, all this bred in him a hardness. To claw back a semblance of self required cultivation of that hardness, fighting early against the grain; an impulse, an iron will *not* to belong. The young mind became attuned to distancing itself. In his novel of 1979, *A Bend in the River*, set in central Africa, it is poignant that the protagonist, Salim, can reflect thus:

So from an early age I developed the habit of looking, detaching myself from a familiar scene and trying to consider it as from a distance. It was from this habit of looking that the idea came to me that as a community we had fallen behind. And that was the beginning of my insecurity. ... I was without the religious sense of my family. The insecurity I felt was due to my lack of true religion...[6]

Naipaul was acquiring the means of self-assessment, astounding powers of observation and attention to detail, but this young mind had had its childhood attenuated. Pessimism came early; laughter did not come easily; when it did it was sardonic. In his novel of 1967, *The Mimic Men*, the protagonist reflects on the void in the childhood:

For Cecil childhood was the great time; he would never cease to regret its passing away. It was different with me. I could scarcely wait for my childhood to be over and done with. I have no especial hardship or deprivation to record. But childhood was for me a period of incompetence, bewilderment, solitude and shameful fantasies. It was a period of burdensome secrets. ... And I longed for nothing so much as to walk in the clear air of adulthood and responsibility, where everything was comprehensible and I myself was open as a book. I hated my secrets. A complying memory has obliterated many of them and edited my childhood down to a brief cinematic blur. Even this is quite sufficiently painful.[7]

The man had come too soon to the child. He lacked a sense of the absurd, which comes out of grounding, belonging, security: roots. Even those works of humour and irony of the early years, 'when the jokes came fast', as he recalled with a touch of self-deprecation, are a cover for an essential pessimism: eschewing the pain of happiness; fostering the hardness so essential to the pursuit of his craft. Yet the certainties of the Brahmin boyhood had residual powers, Naipaul's persistent disavowal notwithstanding. They evoked yearning for that old security, however flawed, in Hindu Trinidad, as he meandered tortuously towards a fragile, constructed English persona.

How hardness gave his way of seeing its pertinacity

I did not have to endure or negotiate those Brahminic certainties. I was not marooned ('shipwrecked') in the Brahmin's universe of rituals and ceremonies; neither did I have to endure people in the mass, day after day, under the same roof. I did not have to take preferential treatment or adulation for granted. I could not become complacent: my people had to earn whatever respect seeped their way, so did I. Therefore, in spite of Naipaul's rejection of his Trinidadian Brahmin roots, it planted in him snobbishness, a lack of manners, a hard certainty, superciliousness with regard to his own intellectual powers and an incapacity for magnanimity or gratitude. Maybe all of this is a mask for an underlying cultural insecurity, but the hardness has kept him going. The hardness has sustained the mission. The hardness has enabled this great mind to work single-mindedly, undeterred by its many detractors, over several decades. It has given the way of seeing its pertinacity.

It can be argued that such seminal instincts of caste superiority, and the accompanying fear of pollution, bred in the man an incapacity for empathy, not only with outsiders, but Indians, too. This has been exacerbated by the thinness and tenuousness of his 'supporting philosophy'. All peoples have a need for rituals; a yearning for communal authentication and reaffirmation of identity, manifested in life-cycle rites, festivals, communal feastings and the commemoration of designated historical events. Naipaul consciously erased these from his own life; he is repelled by the 'wallow' of the 'tribe'; he hates crowds. Yet he would travel widely, in Africa and Asia, to collect material for his books. He would seek out the unclean: he would visit the slums; he would observe Indians chewing, spitting and shitting; he would see the bush taking over, everywhere in Africa; he would admit that he fucked whores regularly. His art has constructed and thrived on a whole 'turd world', to use his late brother Shiva's disparaging play on that concept. It is as if the thinness of his philosophical and cultural moorings needs frailties, fundamental flaws everywhere, in order to validate the self. The vulnerability breeds the dark vision. The empathy is missing, the later narratives saturated with voices of the 'subaltern' notwithstanding; he really cannot relate any more to Indians than to Africans. In 1981, Shiva Naipaul (1945-85) admitted that he himself was 'a very vulnerable construction':

45

If I was like a fish out of water at a Hindu rite, I was no less a fish out of water at a drive-in cinema scented with the vapours of hotdogs and hamburgers. Such definition as I do now possess has its roots in nothing other than personal exigency. As a result, I understand how vulnerable a construction I am.[8]

This needs no revision with regard to Vidia. Out of the private void flows the deficit in generosity and empathy.

In the early 1990s, a Belgian woman, a journalist, tracked Naipaul down, to his sister's house in Trinidad, and eventually procured an interview. Later, they were returning from a drive into the forest and were approaching a rum shop, that institution at the heart of the West Indian gift for talk and laughter. Naipaul could see nothing redeeming in it. He sneered: 'Look at them sitting there. Sitting and drinking.' The woman enjoined perceptively: 'And talking ... I've seen that – the men are always discussing things.' Naipaul put an end to that shaft of illumination: 'Talking! They have nothing on their minds.' He had told her that he hated carnival, the music, the noise: 'I have never danced in my life, not once.' He was out of place; he had little in common with Trinidadians: 'They don't work with the mind. [9]

His experience, beyond 'the fortress' was puny

I knew many years ago that the great mind was missing a lot; the basis of comprehension was flawed. The empathy, crafted by my childhood, does not belong there. His experience beyond the 'fortress', the Brahminic certainties and social conformities, was slight. The talent alone could not fill the void; the travels, later, could not escape the original darkness: Naipaul has had amazing mileage from this second-hand knowledge; but outside of A House for Mr. Biswas, the absence of experience, the thinness of the 'solidity', shows.

I will conclude with an assessment by Andrew Robinson, whose interview of Naipaul I referred to at the start of this piece. It speaks to the power of the man's work whatever one's reservations:

Among the Believers, written in the wake of the Iranian revolution of 1979, was prophetic about the rage of fundamentalist Islam. India: A Million Mutinies Now, published in 1990, was prescient about the sea-change in India of the past decade. ... In both cases, Naipaul's intuitions and indefatigable on-the-spot research were well ahead of the academic reaction. As for the professional study of literature, there are many who would say that Naipaul's diagnosis is today being proved uncomfortably accurate. Naipaul may be savage in his criticisms of academic desiccation, and hardly practical in his solutions to the current malaise in the study of the humanities on both sides of the Atlantic. But no one should make the mistake of imagining that he speaks from mere prejudice. At least this once, the Nobel [P]rize was given to a writer who will always be read – and not just by academics – for his intelligence and insight and for the clarity and elegance of his style.[10]

It was V. S. Naipaul, more than anyone, who gave me the idea that books could be written by Indians in the West Indies. I would play with his books for a little while, flicking through the pages, admiring his picture (with the cigarette in his left hand), astounded by the achievement. I thought the cigarette went with the art of composition. I would smell the fresh print, already evocative of another kind of learning, beyond the tattered, yellowing religious texts of our India-born Brahmin priest. I would hold the book in what I thought was a scholarly fashion, in my right hand with it pressed firmly against my right chest, before the mirror. The reading would come later – slowly, meticulously, with periodic smelling of the print and reassessments of Vidia's picture. But it was his masterpiece, *A House for Mr. Biswas*, which I read around 1964, at the time of our racial troubles in British Guiana, which convinced me that we could write books about ourselves. That idea never left me.

He has, indeed, been a major influence on me. What would I not do for the clarity and elegance of his style? But I never envied him the burden of his genius.

Notes

1. *The Times Higher Education*, 9 August 2002.
2. 'Going back for a Turn in the East' [Andrew Robinson interviews V. S. Naipaul], *The Sunday Times*, 16 September 1990.
3. V. S. Naipaul, 'Two Worlds', Nobel Lecture, 7 December 2001.
4. See note 1.
5. V. S. Naipaul, *The Mimic Men* (London: Andre Deutsch, 1967), p. 73.
6. V. S. Naipaul, *A Bend in the River* (Harmondsworth: Penguin, 1980 [1979]) pp 21-22.

7. V. S. Naipaul. *Finding the Centre: Two Narratives* (London: Andre Deutsch, 1984) p. 109.
8. The *Express* (Trinidad), 20 December 1981.
9. Lieve Joris, 'Home to the snakes and the sensitive plants', *New Statesman*, 17 December 2001.
10. See note 2.

Note on the contributor

Clem Seecharan is Emeritus Professor of History at London Metropolitan University. His *Sweetening 'Bitter Sugar'* received the Elsa Goveia Prize in 2005 from the Association of Caribbean Historians. The second volume of his *Hand-in-Hand: History of Cricket in Guyana* will be published later this year. He is currently writing a book on Cheddi Jagan and the Cold War. Clem was awarded the Doctor of Letters by the University of the West Indies in October 2017. This chapter is drawn from his *Finding Myself: Essays on Race, Politics and Culture* (Leeds: Peepal Tree Press, 2015).

Chapter 5

When a university audience asked the Great Writer to read a happy passage

David Dabydeen (then a new academic) remembers the time Sir Vidia visited Warwick – and the panic V. S. caused simply by asking to use the toilet...

V. S. Naipaul visited the University of Warwick in 1992 to do a reading. The Centre for Caribbean Studies was developing an interest in Indo-Caribbean history and culture. In 1988, on the 150th anniversary of the arrival of Indian indentured labourers into British Guiana, the Centre (years later renamed the Yesu Persaud Centre for Caribbean Studies, after the great Indo-Guyanese philanthropist) had organised the first academic conference in Britain on indentureship and its legacies. Publishers like Macmillan and Hansib were encouraged to acknowledge that the region was not solely an African sphere, but that Indians, Chinese and other peoples had created the Caribbean. If Asians were largely ignored in the historiography of the region, imagine how thin the literature was about the indigenous Amerindian population. That Naipaul had written pungently on India as well as on the decimation of indigenous peoples made his 1992 visit of great significance to the Centre.

I had written to him soon after the publication of *India: A Million Mutinies Now* (1990) and, to my utter surprise, he agreed to come up to Warwick, albeit for a sizeable, but appropriate fee. He phoned to ask what he should be reading from. I suggested *A House For Mr. Biswas (1961),* the great comic novel of the twentieth century, but right away he said no, it was old material. So, it was agreed that he would read from *India: A Million Mutinies Now*. He phoned a second time to confirm arrangements: the Vice-Chancellor was sending his car to collect Naipaul from Wiltshire and deliver him back after the reading event; Naipaul didn't want the car to come to his house, and made an arrangement to be picked up at the railway station; the time of arrival and departure, and other menial matters were decided upon.

On the day itself, there was great nervousness and excitement since Naipaul rarely gave public readings. Many distinguished writers had visited Warwick but none so famous and controversial as Naipaul. The Vice-Chancellor's driver was given a description of Naipaul ('a small, brown-skinned Indian-looking man in a tie and jacket'), warned to address the writer as Sir Vidia and told not to talk to him unless invited to, except to ask him whether he wished to stop at a motorway service station for refreshment and relief. The Caribbean Studies Secretary, hearing that Naipaul was sensitive to dust and dirt, cleaned my office thoroughly and made the teacups gleam. I told all my colleagues that they were forbidden to come to my office whilst Naipaul was there, in case they said something that Naipaul took exception to: we had all read that he was very sensitive and was liable to walk out if offended. When Naipaul did arrive, he asked to use the toilet. There was panic on my part: there is no staff toilet at Warwick, otherwise I would have cleaned it and locked it for his coming. Academics used the same toilets as students, and as I took Naipaul there, I dreaded the prospect of some unflushed faecal matter left behind by some idle person, or toilet seats wet with urine. We had all read about his obsession with the scatological. I waited outside, out of fright more than respect, and was utterly relieved when I heard him washing his hands and when he emerged without a scowl.

Humbling and terrifying in the presence of Naipaul

An hour of isolation in my office followed, before his event, for he had arrived earlier than planned. I was then a relatively new and young academic, with a couple of slim volumes of verse to my credit, all that I was worth in the world. To be in the presence of Naipaul, without recourse to escape, was greatly humbling and terrifying. I began by asking him why he had accepted my invitation to Warwick. He said his wife had asked him the very same question when he set off! He said he, himself, was surprised at his agreement to read. A few minutes later, he asked me about Canada, and I realised that he had mistaken me for my cousin, Cyril Dabydeen, a poet in Ottawa and an acquaintance of Naipaul's nephew, the writer Neil Bissoondath. Naipaul had come to Warwick possibly out of obligation to his nephew. I kept quiet, I didn't want him to leave.

I began to ask him about India, and Indians in the Caribbean, but before I could, he sprung to his feet and extracted a book on Michel-Jean Cazabon from my shelf. Cazabon (1813-1888) was Trinidad's greatest, and only internationally known, painter. Apart from the landscape of Trinidad, Cazabon painted indentured Indians. Naipaul flicked through the book and in no time located the watercolour entitled 'East Indian Group'. It showed a proud-looking and dignified Indian, with a handsome and well-kept moustache staring at the viewer without any sign of weakness or awareness of being of lowly status; his young, comely, bejewelled wife; his equally charming young daughter. To be sure, they posed before a thatched hut, but Cazabon has given it a rustic charm, not a signifier of poverty. 'This picture belongs to me,' he said proudly, holding up the illustration to me so I could examine it, and the inscription which read: 'Collection Vidia Naipaul.'

He had been a little sombre up to then, and bored, but now he lit up. It was moving to me, to appreciate suddenly that for all Naipaul's scathing criticisms of India and Trinidad, the love which suffused *Biswas* was as powerful as ever. Right away, I blurted out how, as an Indo-Caribbean youth, I was astonished and moved to deep laughter and deep sadness and deep gratitude, when I read *Biswas*. He didn't respond: the novel was truly old material for him. So, I asked him, instead, about his recent article on Cheddi Jagan, in which Jagan was spared from scathing description and dismissal. 'Is it because he was the first Indo-Caribbean political leader that you wrote kindly about him?' I asked sheepishly. Naipaul shook his head. 'No, no, no,' he chided me. 'It is because Jagan is sincere.' He looked at the bookshelf again, and noticed many novels by Wilson Harris. 'What do you think of Harris?' he asked. I searched for an intelligent response, mumbling something about the mystical aspects of the writing. When I paused, he said coldly: 'I have never read Harris.'

Fortunately, after fifteen minutes or so, an Indian photographer, Prodeepta Das, knocked on the door. I had asked Naipaul whether a few photographs could be taken of him, to mark the occasion of his visit. He refused, but after further entreaty, agreed to one photograph. Prodeepta Das duly took one photograph. When Naipaul learnt he was from Orissa, he right away engaged Das in conversation about art and culture in Orissa, and I was spared from having to keep Naipaul's solitary company and to further expose my extreme nervousness. Fifteen minutes later, a student knocked on the door by prior arrangement. I had asked Naipaul whether he would sign copies of his novels, but he refused. 'I will sign one,' he said. And the student duly got one copy signed, leaving the office in haste and perplexed.

'Being sixty is nothing to celebrate'

As we walked across campus to the lecture theatre, I was bold enough to ask Naipaul whether I could interview him on another occasion, to mark his 60th birthday. He paused and shook his head. 'Being sixty is nothing to celebrate. My friend turned sixty recently and I was sorry for her!' And then he tilted his face to catch the light and invited me to look at his skin, as he had invited me to look at the Cazabon. 'I detest interviews. So stressful. Can you see how scaly it is? I broke out in rashes soon after I did an interview the other day with that boy ... that boy ...' He struggled as if to remember the name of the 'boy'. Of course, he meant the brilliant and charismatic Farrukh Dhondy, known to the world for his Channel Four commissioning, but Naipaul was being provocative, knowing full well that one day I would tell the story (knowing full well that, being a great writer, anyone he spoke to would store up anecdotes). I began to think that not only was he easily bored by the likes of me (too timid to engage with him rewardingly), but he had to keep himself interested by being provocative, so as to get a response... In Trinidad, such banter and mockery ('picong') is ingrained.

The Vice-Chancellor, Clark Brundin, chaired the event. He was in genuine awe of Naipaul. He began a long, adulatory introduction. Naipaul beckoned to me. I went up to him. 'I cannot read,' he whispered. 'I have left my reading glasses in the Vice-Chancellor's office. My briefcase. The middle compartment.' I walked out of the lecture theatre calmly, then scooted to the Vice-Chancellor's office nearby, rushed up the stairs, regretting that years of cigarette smoking had winded me, found the briefcase, opened it. What an honour, this task of retrieving his reading glasses! There it was, in the middle compartment. I noticed about a dozen bottles of medicine in the right-hand compartment and a typescript in the left-hand compartment. I wish I had had time to peep at the typescript but, instead, rushed back to the lecture theatre and handed the reading glasses to Naipaul just as the Vice-Chancellor was finishing his oration.

Naipaul began lively, explaining how he came to write *India: A Million Mutinies Now*, and how he decided to be like a living tape recorder, allowing people to tell their own stories with minimal interruption on his part. It promised to be a fascinating talk on the process of travel writing, when a photographer from the local *Coventry Evening Telegraph* suddenly emerged in the middle of the lecture theatre, paused for many seconds, took aim and clicked, the flash seeming to blind Naipaul. He stopped. His face creased. He was deciding whether to walk out. The photographer and bright flash had disrupted his thinking. After what seemed an eternity, he resumed. 'As you all know, I am not a lecturer. I have to prepare my mind carefully for an address like this...' The audience of hundreds understood, and the hostility to the photographer was palpable. Naipaul, sensing he had the sympathy of the audience, decided to continue, He began to read from *India*. After the first passage, greeted with loud applause, he brightened. 'Now, do you want a happy passage, or a tragic one. You choose,' he told the audience. 'Happy,' they shouted, no doubt surprised that Naipaul was capable of such, given his reputation for biting satire. He read again, at length. He was enjoying himself, enjoying his performance.

'Why do they give me their books?'

Afterwards, I ushered him out of the theatre before people could crowd him. As we left the building, heading for the Vice-Chancellor's office, a man was wheeled up to meet him. It was the Indian writer, Firdaus Kanga. He was a small bundle of flesh. He held out his book, *Heaven on Wheels* (1990), a wonderfully readable and provocative narrative of Kanga's journey through Britain on a wheelchair, in which he expressed fervent admiration for Thatcherism. 'I would like to present my book to you, Sir Vidia,' he said in his squeaky voice. Naipaul looked shocked. He would not take the book. I did so, on his behalf. Before we entered the Vice-Chancellor's office, he stopped and asked me: 'Why do they give me their books?' (Years later, we all read about his getting rid of Theroux's book of 1968, *Fong and the Indians*). I wanted to tell him the obvious, which was that he was so revered that other writers were thrilled just to have him possess one of their works; and I wanted to remind him that his first major literary, paid endeavour was commenting on other people's books as a presenter of the BBC's *Caribbean Voices* programme. Before I could speak, he asked: 'If they were dancers, would they dance for me?' I don't think this question was referring to Kanga, who suffered from brittle bones, but it was an odd one.

The Vice-Chancellor had organised a reception for a dozen or so scholars. Naipaul didn't want to meet them, but was eventually persuaded to do so. One of them, who had written extensively on Trinidad and whose academic career was partly based on such research, asked him why he had stopped writing about the country. Drily he answered: 'Because it is not important.'

A brilliant, if cruel, dismissal of an academic career, though Naipaul was not to know!

Naipaul would not attend the dinner the Vice-Chancellor had organised in his honour. Maybe he was tired. Maybe he shunned groups of strangers. Maybe he didn't enjoy the company of academics. Maybe he wanted privacy, having exposed himself to the audience. Maybe he wanted to dine in private. Maybe eating with low-caste and non-caste strangers was inimical to a Brahmin. Who knows? I gathered up his briefcase to take him to the waiting car. I gave him Kanga's book. He refused it. 'You keep it,' he said. Today I still have in my possession *Heaven on Wheels*, with its heartfelt inscription thanking Naipaul for being such an inspiration to Kanga and other writers.

A year later, at a lunch organised by the Arts Council to celebrate Naipaul's winning of the David Cohen Prize, fifteen of us, judges and guests, sat around the dining table. Apart from Naipaul, I was the only person of colour in the room. Of course, he ignored me and, out of respect for him, I did not seek his gaze or look directly at him. He made a speech heaping scorn on some writer of biography whose name escapes me. Afterwards, the room emptied. I stayed back for a minute or so to finish the fine wine, when Naipaul suddenly walked in. He had forgotten to sign the guests' book. There were only the two of us, sharing an uncomfortable space. 'Will you come back to Warwick when you are free to do another reading?' I asked for want of something more intelligent to say. He looked at me fiercely and pointed to his leg. 'I developed a limp soon after I left Warwick. It bothered me for months. You caused it.' I remembered the bottles of pills in his briefcase, his accusation against the 'boy' for blighting his skin ... all innocent, given his hypochondria. I really didn't mind his insult. I think he relished being galling, and creating a nasty persona and putting distance between himself and voyeurs (in his mind literary critics, journalists, etc). By all accounts he was a cruel man, but he had greatness in him, and what mattered was the writing, not the person or persona.

Note on the contributor

David Dabydeen was born in British Guiana. He read English at Cambridge and has been an academic at the University of Warwick for more than 30 years. Between 2010 and 2015 he was Guyana's Ambassador to China. He has published seven novels and two collections of poetry.

Chapter 6

He was the all-seeing, inner eye that witnessed inconvenient truths

V. S. Naipaul was quintessentially a West Indian intellectual, struggling with the contradictory consciousness of post-colonialism, argues Sir Hilary Beckles.

V. S. Naipaul, our phenomenal West Indian son, has left behind a substantial space in our society that we can only hope will one day be filled again. Indeed, the tributes have been marked with sadness on all sides of the discursive divide of the subject he focused on with sensational success—the naked and hidden truths of the post-colonial world. West Indian society was blessed to have produced and unleashed him upon a world much in need of self-liberation.

For over half a century the master scribe was magisterial in pursuit of his mission. All who read and heard him marvelled at his intellectual insights, though his panache for pinching the raw nerve extracted fury from a few. The mega-narrative of the literary icon was the primary inner theme of our times—freedom. Imagining a legitimate literary 'West Indianness' was for him, at times, nothing more than frivolity; more meaningful were the possibilities embedded in the ontologies of ancestry.

He reserved his satirical sting for the emerging societies of what he termed the 'bourgeois banana democracies' that proliferated on the peripheries of empire. Migration, he said, the brick and mortar of the West Indies, had made us all mad as we imagined the attainment of freedom from colonial ideals. The very idea of 'madness' proved to be a metaphor of nationhood embedded in Naipaulian dimensions.

From *Biswas* to *Mimic Men*, the West Indian journey to justice is narrated in the contradictory pains and passions of our attempts to detach and depart from the colonial scaffold. Naipaul was not confident in the sincerity and integrity of the detachment and, as a result, delved deeply and described the political brutality, cultural banality and heroic vanity of the effort.

In many respects Naipaul was the all-seeing, inner eye that witnessed inconvenient truths daily brushed under a mountainous Caribbean rug. V. S. was very special in every sense. His 'Trini' roots were as deep as can be imagined; every branch of his work drew upon Indian springs that fertilised his Caribbean comprehension of the ontological encounter so lyrically captured as the Nile-Ganges discourse.

Inserting this indigenous Caribbean mindscape into the open field of British imperial brutishness provided the core of his global view about the world and everyone's place in it. He admitted to adoring aspects of Englishness and was contemptuous of 'creole' versions of it, a pivot that drew attention to popular mimicry. His cravings for notions of essence led him to experiencing 'home' as nothing more than ruins filled with 'despair and rootlessness'. Redemption and, less so, reparations were not items on his radar.

Our literary genius was quintessentially a West Indian intellectual, struggling with the contradictory consciousness of post-colonialism, including the parodies and pleasures of imperial culture. He was torn and tortured at every turn, and never sought to find solace or inner peace in any conciliatory conceptual discourse. Instead, he dug deeper into the reality he felt could not be repaired. Home, he felt, was filled with pain, and now he will never return to it again.

Writing provided the inspirational use of his abundant existential turbulence and served as a cocoon for his complex, hyper-critical consciousness. Without words and ideas, he would have long ceased to be. His persistent melancholy was as West Indian as cricket, carnival and picong. He will dwell amongst us for ever. We bid farewell and send blessings to accompany him to ancestors. Here resides the great V. S. Naipaul, in a special way, the St. Paul of Caribbean civilisation.

Note on the contributor

Professor Sir Hilary Beckles, an economic historian, was installed as the 8th Vice-Chancellor of the University of the West Indies on 30 May 2015. Before that, he was Principal and Pro Vice-Chancellor of the University's Cave Hill Campus in Barbados for 13 years (2002-2015). Sir Hilary is a distinguished university administrator and transformational leader in higher education.

For his complete biography see http://www.uwi.edu/VCBiography.asp.

This article first appeared at
https://www.mona.uwi.edu/marcom/newsroom/entry/7086.

Chapter 7

Mr. Ford's hacienda

Tariq Ali remembers his times discussing with Naipaul the possible screen adaptation of his autobiographical A House for Mr. Biswas and tells of novelist's previous meeting with a celebrated Hollywood director...

V. S. Naipaul never saw himself as just another face in the mural of 20th-century literature. The mural was, in any case, not his favourite art form. He loved and possessed a very fine collection of Persian and Indian miniatures. But this wasn't a frame in which he saw himself either. Long before the knighthood and the Nobel Prize, it was the mirror that excited him. Destiny stared him in the face every morning. He believed in himself. The Trinidadian was to become a very fine writer of English prose.

Naipaul and C. L. R. James were educated at the same colonial school. The high quality of teaching in classics and English literature left its mark on both men. Both of them came to England. There the similarity ends. James moved to Marxism and became a great historian in that tradition. Naipaul put politics on the back-burner, joined the lesser ranks of vassalage (the BBC) and cultivated a cultural conservatism that later became his hallmark both politically and socially. The classical heritage of the European bourgeoisie had completely bewitched him. He saw it as the dominant pillar of Western civilisation and this led him to underplay, ignore and sometimes to justify its barbaric sides both at home and abroad.

In later years, James (in private conversation) would refer to Naipaul as someone who was often needed in an imperialist country trying to create a post-colonial culture so as to say things about native peoples that are no longer acceptable in polite society. Naipaul was never, by any stretch of the imagination, a card-carrying Tory. He lived his life through a circle of friends that he had carefully selected. Most, if not all, were figures on the right.

Whatever his politics, the novels were very good, especially the earlier ones. His first, the autobiographical *A House for Mr. Biswas*, remains a comic masterpiece. And it would have made an excellent TV series, or so I thought. Would he ever agree? It wasn't a secret that Naipaul had long opposed his work being transferred to small or big screen. Twenty-odd years ago I rang him up and was invited to lunch. He confirmed that he had always hated the idea of his work being polluted by cinema or television and told me how his excited US agent had once forced him to fly out to 'Mr. Ford's hacienda' to discuss filming *A Bend in the River*. 'Mr. Ford' was his name for Francis Ford Coppola.

Against his own instincts, Naipaul arrived on the West Coast. At the hacienda, Coppola informed him that the only other guest apart from family would be George Lucas. Naipaul was amazed. 'Georg Lukács, the Hungarian philosopher? I thought he was dead?' It got worse. During supper Coppola handed Naipaul a script that he had commissioned. He wanted Naipaul to have a quick read of the adaptation and see what he thought. While handing the script, 'Mr Ford was also trying to swallow some spaghetti which he managed to spill on his shirt. It was a very vulgar occasion. I decided to leave.' Which he did. Since then, he had turned down every proposal.

His second wife, Nadira, whom he married in 1996, persuaded him to calm down and let Ismail Merchant commission Caryl Phillips to write a script of *The Mystic Masseur*. Naipaul was filled with foreboding that it might turn out to be awful. 'It did.' This was not a promising start. He asked why I liked *A House for Mr. Biswas*. 'It's pure,' I replied, 'and very funny.' He agreed we should have a go. Farrukh Dhondy, he agreed, knew the book well and Channel Four commissioned the scripts. Peter Ansorge was a stern invigilator and made sure that most of the dialogue from the novel was retained. When we discussed the scripts and possible directors over dinner at my place several months later, Naipaul, Nadira and Gillon Aitken (his agent) were pleased with the final product.

Channel Four had appointed a new boss who had brought in a new drama editor, Gub Neal, who also liked the scripts. But the marketing folk at the channel were surprised to discover that no white star could be cast in a main role, since there was none in the novel. No black stars either except in minor roles. It was Trinidadian Asians all the way through, a 'problem' that would never have bothered Satyajit Ray or Ken Loach. And so the project was cancelled. Naipaul was shocked but not surprised. The scripts still work and if Ian Katz seriously wants to lift Channel Four a tiny bit from the ratings sewer where it has been immersed for many years, he might have a read.

Note on the contributor

Tariq Ali's latest book is *The Dilemmas of Lenin, Terrorism, War, Empire, Love, Revolution* (Verso). This article first appeared at https://www.lrb.co.uk/blog/2018/08/13/tariq-ali/mr-fords-hacienda/.

Section 2

Trinidad: a love/hate relationship with his 'homeland'

John Mair

Naipaul was born in Chaguanas in the South of Trinidad and grew up in the capital, Port of Spain. His relationship with his 'homeland' afterwards was tortuous, ambivalent, sometimes resentful. He was lauded by the government and by the academe in Trinidad. But V. S. did not always reciprocate. He once called it 'half-formed'.

To understand Trinidad you have to understand its history. Like Guyana, it is riven with ethnic conflict dating back to the nineteenth century. The black slaves were freed from the sugar estates in 1838 to be replaced by Indian indentured labourers brought in from Uttar Pradesh and Bihar. They initially laboured in the sugar fields but their natural entrepreneurialism took them towards owning land and then cultivating it for sustenance and cash crops. Later they moved into commerce and the professions – traditionally 'black' domains leading to jealousy and conflict between the races. It is still there. Governments alternate between the brown and black parties. The winner takes it all.

The island economy was based on the cultivation of sugar. That has all but died out. It was replaced by the discovery of oil offshore. That industry, too, is dying. Now ammonia and natural gas keep Trinidad industrialised.

Parts of the island, especially in the South, are 'Little Indias'. Temples, *hanomans*, the food, music and baubles of 'Mother India' are there but with a firmly Caribbean flavour. The cuisine and the people have adapted to new spices. It was to the bazaar bustle of Chaguanas that V. S. was born. While his mother came from a prosperous family, his father was a mere journalist on a national paper – and that created tension. Soon they moved to Port of Spain and to the road that was thinly disguised as *Miguel Street* in his book of that name. As the East Indians urbanised, some of their traditions and language were left behind. Multi culturalism ruled.

By the middle of the twentieth century, the 'East Indians' (as they were accurately called) were moving their progeny into the professions and commerce and the mighty West Indian cricket teams of the time. Their route was education and especially QRC – the Queen's Royal College. Even here, Naipaul stood out from his contemporaries – as Lloyd Best shows in his essay here:

I have a clear picture of my first encounter, sometime in 1945. It was during the last minutes before the mid-day resumption. I'd sneaked upstairs from Third to Sixth Form. Not the done thing. …. That lunch break, for some reason, it seemed especially animated in heaven. It was the first time I'd ever tiptoed up, promptly to be chased. But there I'd glimpsed him on the balcony, in khaki shorts, Cambridge blue shirt, standing and holding court. It is the image that lasts.

Naipaul shone brightest among the bright stars of QRC: brown, black and white. He won a Trinidad Scholarship to study abroad. And so V. S. was off to England and Oxford University. He was never to return to live in Trinidad. His Trini years, though, provided the basis for his early works, especially *A House for Mr. Biswas* for which read *A House for Mr. Naipaul (Senior)*.

Naipaul and 'the country of the mind'

Professor Kenneth Ramchand is the foremost Naipaul scholar in Trinidad. His contribution on 'Did Naipaul hate Trinidad?' is a masterly piece of work written especially for this book. Thorough, thoughtful and full of follow-up lines. It starts with Naipaul's famous line:

History is built around achievement and creation; and nothing was created in the West Indies.

And then the essay drills down to his view of Trinidad (the second largest 'British' island in the West Indies) and his ennui about it. According to Ramchand, Naipaul's comments on Africans, Indians and political unity:

> ... have roused strong emotions as is usually the case when race and colour are part of the subject. The rumour took wing among Indians that Naipaul hated them. And, of course, he hated Africans too. These are subsets of hating Trinidad.

Many commentators, some in this volume, lambast Naipaul for his 'anti-Trinidad' rants. Ramchand is kinder to him than many:

> Trinidad was the truth that kept interrupting the effort to belong elsewhere that Naipaul made in *The Enigma of Arrival*. He feared and therefore hated the social, cultural and political pressures in island society and family life that threatened the writer with extinction.

Ramchand concludes both movingly and firmly:

> It might be difficult to ever convince those who hate him as being anti-Trinidad that he wrote out of a love for the island of his birth, wrote to help it achieve the self-knowledge that would set it free. Thomas Aquinas knew that V. S. Naipaul needed someone who understood: 'Nothing is hated, save through being contrary to a suitable thing which is loved. And hence it is that every hatred is caused by love.' The country of the mind is the model of the 'suitable thing' that Naipaul loved.

His obsession: 'How do I find my way in the world?'

Professor Kirk Meighoo is not far behind Professor Ramchand in the Naipaul scholarship stakes. He places V. S. firmly in the Caribbean:

> There is no person who has written more on Trinidad, for a longer period of time, to a wider audience than V. S. Naipaul ... Naipaul had one obsessive concern: 'How do I, as a Trinidad Indian, born in this small colony, isolated from the rest of the world, marginal even here, find my way in the world?' It was the great theme of his life's work.

Professor Bridget Brereton, the distinguished Trinidadian historian, says of V. S. that whatever he may have said (or failed to say) about Trinidad, 'even when he was being deliberately mischievous, no one should doubt that he was, indeed, created right here'.

Finally, as the Caribbeans say: 'I was baarn here. Me navel string is buried here.' So too Naipaul's in Trinidad. Whether he liked it or not.

Chapter 8

Did Naipaul hate Trinidad?

Through a detailed examination of Naipaul's writings, Kenneth Ramchand argues that V. S actually wrote out of a love for the island of his birth – to help it achieve the self-knowledge that would set it free.

Prelude: a story with a moral – Did James Joyce hate Ireland?

James Joyce left Ireland in 1904 when he was 22 years old. He returned briefly on three occasions but he never set foot in Ireland after 1912. Church and state hated him. On his death in 1941, his wife's offer to repatriate his body was refused, and the government instructed its ambassador not to attend the funeral.

Joyce hated and poured scorn on what he saw as the outlandish and confused politics and the backward cultural agenda of his country. He hated Catholicism for destroying individuality and creating decadence. Dublin was 'the centre of paralysis'.

Joyce also feared Dublin. He wanted to escape from it. If he stayed he would end up like the failed writer Gabriel Conroy in the story 'The Dead' (*Dubliners*, 1914). He feared Ireland as a place that consumed its artists and other creative people. 'You know what Ireland is?' he allowed the character, Stephen Dedalus, to declare in *Portrait of the Artist As a Young Man* (1916). 'Ireland is the old sow that eats her farrow [newborn litter].'

Dublin was, nevertheless, the physical setting of all his work, and it was the begetter of everything he wrote, including *Ulysses* (1922) and *Finnegan's Wake* (1939). He never disengaged from what he condemned. There is no more realistic and imaginative rendering of the Dublin of Joyce's formative years, its streets, its voices, its music and its spirit. Joyce left Dublin, but Dublin never left him. In the final reckoning, he loved Ireland and wanted it to find itself. This is where he stood: 'Welcome, O life! I go to encounter for the millionth time the reality of experience, and to forge in the smithy of my soul the uncreated conscience of my race.'

Joyce hated and feared Dublin, but he wrote about it all the time. He wanted to encounter the reality of experience and he wanted to forge the uncreated conscience of his race. Only a kind of love would have made him want to do that and to declare:

'When I die, Dublin will be written in my heart.'

Hate is complex in its manifestations and in its origins. Iago's malignity in Shakespeare's *Othello* is a wrathful and diabolic hate that wants to destroy only for the sake of destruction. Can we ever know where hate like that comes from? Thankfully, it is not that kind of hate that we are thinking about here. If the word 'hate' is to be used with reference to V. S. Naipaul's attitudes to Trinidad, it would have to be classed as the kind of hate described by St Thomas Aquinas:

Nothing is hated, save through being contrary to a suitable thing which is loved. And hence it is that every hatred is caused by love.

In this exploration of V. S. Naipaul's 'cleansing-of-the-temple' attitudes to Trinidad, the case of James Joyce stands as a useful precedent.

'Nothing was created in the West Indies'

Naipaul's justly deplored omission of the name of Trinidad from his list of acknowledgements on being awarded the Nobel Prize for literature in 2001 served as a reminder of an imagined wound that still festers. One sentence in *The Middle Passage* (1962) has become notorious for inflicting that wound. It is cited by all who want to indict Naipaul for being anti-West Indian and for hating Trinidad. The sentence is reproduced even for those who know it by heart:

History is built around achievement and creation; and nothing was created in the West Indies.

The sentence comes at the end of a nationalistic discussion (*The Middle Passage* pp 27, 28 and 29) of the attitudes and behaviours of the Europeans who bossed slave society. With the help of telling quotations from British witnesses, Naipaul tags plantation whites as low-life, cruel and violent to those below them; as creatures with coarse appetites and vulgar sensualities; people with no learning, no interest in the arts and sciences;

beings with no life of the mind, no idea of civilisation; creatures with no instinct to make a home of the place to which they had come.

The sentence does not imply denial or denigration of the folk culture of the enslaved and indentured peoples; or of the history of survival and resistance; or of the astounding outbursts of creativity and self-expression in song, story, calypso, dance, music, religion, festivals and carnival in the closing decades of nineteenth century Trinidad. Naipaul's sentence is nothing to do with that. Nor is it a comment on twentieth century Trinidad. The sentence is nothing more than part of a complaint about the whites in slave society. It is restated forty-five years later on p. 24 of *A Writer's People* (2007):

> Europe had left behind nothing that could be called a civilisation, no great architecture, no idea of local beauty, no memory of style and splendour, nothing a man would wish to call his own.

If 'Nothing was created' is read in context it can be seen as a sentence in what was an implicit plea for us to discover and write our own history and build our own ships.

Professor Elsa Goveia's brilliant *Slave Society in the British Leeward Islands at the End of the Eighteenth Century* (1965) defined the island societies as slave societies whose history could not be written and whose inner dynamics could not be understood if the shaping presence of slaves and free blacks was treated as peripheral. This dispassionate, scholarly and ground-breaking book inspired West Indian historians to turn research attention to the voiceless, nameless slave and to describe and analyse the hidden/suppressed cultures of the islands. Naipaul was clearly moving in this direction in *The Middle Passage* which appeared three years before Goveia's seminal contribution. By the time we come to the Epilogue to *The Loss of El Dorado* (1969), he calls – as does Wilson Harris in *History Fable and Myth in the Caribbean and the Guianas* (1970) – for an imaginative and researched history that would reconstruct the lives of the faceless, storyless, voiceless natives:

> Port of Spain was a place where things had happened and nothing showed. Only people remained. History was a fairytale about Columbus and a fairytale about the strange customs of the aboriginal Caribs and Arawaks; it was impossible now to set them in the landscape. History was the Trinidad five-cent stamp; Raleigh

discovering the Pitch lake. History was also a fairytale not so much about slavery as about its abolition, the good defeating the bad. It was the only way the tale could be told. Any other version would have ended in ambiguity and alarm. The slave as slave was never real. Like the extinct aboriginal, he had to be reconstructed from his daily routine. So he remains, existing, like Vallot's jail (of which no plan survives), only in the imagination. In the records, the slave is faceless, silent, with an identification rather than a name. He has no story.

Will there ever be a non-partisan and rational discussion in the West Indies of 'Nothing was created'?

Sounding *The Middle Passage*

The whole account of Trinidad in Chapter 2 of *The Middle Passage* has been held by some in the West Indies to provide detailed evidence of hatred of Trinidad and of the author's negative views of people of African origin. There are earlier tremors and symptoms, in Naipaul's fiction and in interviews, but this eruption came in 1962 with the publication of *The Middle Passage*. Trinidad was struck hard. The book reaches back to Naipaul's childhood, and its aftershocks are to be felt well into his later years. The first reason why *The Middle Passage* hits so hard, and makes people feel aggrieved, is because it chooses what to hit. It leaves alone many qualities of Trinidad and Trinidadians who make it a lovable country. Re-readings of *The Middle Passage*, even in tranquillity, do not change the fact that Naipaul, in the book, is critical of the condition of Trinidad. But it is striking now to see in it how many positive things Naipaul says *en passant* about Trinidad and Trinidadians: the palpable energy in the air, the lust for life, the warmth and kindness of strangers, the natural anarchism and free self-expression of the Trinidadian. These are positive aspects that make the criticisms sound not like a rant but as something felt with sorrow and a sense of possibilities wasted.

It cannot be denied that the chapter on Trinidad leaves out positive aspects that Naipaul did not see, and does not emphasise some that he did see. What the seeing eye and darting mind took in, however, the pen sets before us with skill and style. It is distressing that the failings the book discerned are still with us; and the evils it uncovers are present fifty years later, in terrifyingly more virulent and extreme form. Today, Trinidadians are literally on the run; those who are abroad come back for a holiday with their return passage booked, or indulge in mainly food-based rituals to concoct a manageable Trinidad in the safe places where they reside. Those who stay know what Naipaul knew from early: there is nowhere to go. 'Oh England is a pleasant place for them that's rich and high,' says the old buccaneer. 'Nah leaving,' sings the calypsonian. Naipaul constructed his own private and largely unrecognised way of accepting home with its sorrows.

The early part of this discussion highlights four of the issues about Trinidad that are raised in *The Middle Passage*, all of them more or less accepted as true by Trinidadians, some being diverted by the humour, and some of them responding angrily – seeing it as ridicule. The issues are:

- the criticism of Trinidadians' 'modernity';
- the description of Trinidad as a picaroon society;
- the lack of nationalism;
- the absence of African-Indian unity;
- and, finally, a surprising one which I have titled 'Naipaul's solutions'.

Naipaul's descriptions of the things he hates are sharp and vivid. The things he hates prevent the society from being a society, and they do all manner of violence to the individual. There can be no doubt from his presentation, however, that he is interested in reform, so much so that he offers a number of practical suggestions about how this might come about. Certain notes are sounded that insinuate, at this stage, a concern that is a matter of life and death. The things that Naipaul hates endanger every individual, none more so than a boy in colonial Trinidad determined to make his way into the literary world, the larger world out there. To Naipaul it amounts to threatening the writer with extinction.

Trinidadians' modernity

Trinidad's self-satisfaction with its 'modernity' is analysed as an escape from reality. It is 'a constant alertness, a willingness to change, a readiness to accept anything which films, magazines, and comic strips appear to indicate as American' (*The Middle Passage* p. 46). To be modern is 'to ignore local products' and to have a preference for foreign: 'bad English potatoes' instead of yams and plantains. This modernity 'turns out to be the extreme susceptibility of people who are unsure of themselves and, having no taste or style of their own, are eager for instruction'. They drink deeply – intoxicated by commercial radio jingles, the advertising agencies, and the other harbingers of American materialism. Naipaul, the satirist, calls it a life of fantasy and asserts that the fantasy is 'cheating' and 'masochistic'. In this work, Naipaul wants to save the society and notably, the calypso which he recognises as a valuable tool in the search for self-knowledge: 'It is only in the calypso that the Trinidadian touches reality.' Even as he says so, however, he laments that the integrity and the social function of the native form are being undermined by self-caricaturing attempts to live up to 'the ideals of the tourist brochure'.

Naipaul's solutions

It is surprising the number of times that Naipaul offers solutions to our plight. With respect to our so-called modernity, he laments our failure to look at ourselves critically, or to look inwards or to re-discover the past: 'Though we knew that something was wrong with our society, we made no attempt to assess it. Trinidad was too unimportant and we could never be convinced of the value of reading the history of a place which was, as everyone said, only a dot on the map of the world. Our interest was all in the world outside. ... Our own past was buried and no one cared to dig it up' (*The Middle Passage* pp 41-42). Later in the chapter, after describing the society as a picaroon society, there is a remarkable burst of youthful sermonising.

To bring political organisation to the picaroon society, with its taste for corruption and violence and its lack of respect for the person, has its dangers. Such a society cannot immediately become responsible; but it can be re-educated only through responsibility. Change must come from the top. Capital punishment and corporal punishment, incitements to brutality, must be abolished. The civil service must be rejuvenated.

He then sketches out a code of conduct for civil servants, people serving the public in business places, in drugstores and even the police: 'The policeman will see that he is more than a licensed bully' and all along the line no one will feel the need 'to display his authority by aggression' (*The Middle Passage* pp 74-75). Finally, having conscripted the calypso into the educational process, he turns to the responsibility of the writer. They have a tendency to flatter the prejudices of their group but they must check up on themselves. They can do better: 'Living in a borrowed culture, the West Indian, more than most, needs writers to tell him who he is and where he stands' (ibid p. 68).

How can anyone have reviewed this book under the title, 'A pageant of apathy'?

Not anancy but the picaroon

Shunning the anancy trope of West Indian writers in which the witty survival skills of trickster anancy are given more emphasis than the cruelty and violence he suffers, the author of *Miguel Street* looks at the trickery, violence, brutality and sentimentality around him and defines the society as one in which slavery, the mixed population, the absence of national pride and the closed colonial system have re-created 'the attitudes of the Spanish picaroon world'.

A frightening place: 'This was an ugly world, a jungle, where the picaroon hero starved unless he stole, was beaten almost to death when found out, and had therefore to get in his blows first whenever possible; where the weak were humiliated; where [Kafka-esquely], the powerful never appeared and were beyond reach ['Tell Me Who to Kill']; where no one was allowed any dignity and everyone had to impose himself; an uncreative society where war was the only profession.' This is one of the sources of the nightmare of being stranded in Trinidad that haunted Naipaul throughout his career. Yet he can value the tolerance produced by the picaroon society ('How could one wish it otherwise?'); this tolerance is not the tolerance between castes and creeds which he insists does not exist on the island, but 'something more profound: tolerance for every human activity, and affection for every demonstration of wit and style' (*The Middle Passage* pp 76-77).

The lack of nationalism

To the Naipaul of *The Middle Passage*, every clique saw itself as the elite, every individual was a guerrilla fighting his own war. Nobody had any loyalty to anything larger than himself – neither family, nor ethnic group, nor region, nor country. Each guerrilla was fighting for his place in the community, yet there was no community:

We were of various races, religions, sets and cliques; and we had somehow found ourselves on the same small island. Nothing bound us together except this common residence. There was no nationalist feeling. … There was no profound anti-imperialist feeling; indeed, it was only our Britishness, our belonging to the British Empire which gave us any identity (*The Middle Passage* p. 43).

When adult suffrage came in 1946, entrepreneurial individuals entered the lists because they saw 'prodigious commercial possibilities'. Naipaul did not add that they were succeeded by the biggest entrepreneurial entity of all, the modern political party. Naipaul sounds in these pages as if he could join a nationalist group fighting to turn a set of peoples into a people.

African-Indian unity

There is no ambivalence in any of Naipaul's attitudes in his comments on the topics in the previous sections. Where there was disagreement about any of his pronouncements on any of the topics, it was rational and not *ad hominem*. But the author's comments on Africans, Indians and political unity have roused strong emotions as is usually the case when race and colour are part of the subject. The rumour took wing among Indians that Naipaul hated them. And, of course, he hated Africans too. These are subsets of hating Trinidad.

When Naipaul comes to discuss the two major ethnic groups on the island, the private anxieties and personal tensions sometimes sensed just below the choppy surface of *The Middle Passage* cannot be missed. Of the Indians of Trinidad, he generalises thus:

> A peasant-minded, money-minded community, spiritually static because cut off from its roots, its religion reduced to rites without philosophy, set in a materialistic colonial society; a combination of historical accidents and national temperament has turned the Trinidad Indian into the complete colonial, even more philistine than the white (*The Middle Passage* p. 82).

This harsh dismissal of the Indians of Trinidad has some justice in it as a description of how things were. Not surprisingly, it led to cries by Indians that Naipaul hated them and, therefore, also hated himself. The severity of the tone suggests that Naipaul is attempting to distance himself from connections that, in the colonial society of his boyhood, were shaming, and full of threats to the self he wanted to become. The family organisation of the Indian was 'an enclosing self-sufficient world absorbed with its quarrels and jealousies, as difficult for the outsider to penetrate as for one of its members to escape. It protected and imprisoned, a static world awaiting decay' (ibid p. 82). To the boy who wanted to become a writer, the Indian connection was entombment from birth.

Naipaul's analysis of the descendants of enslaved African peoples was done before the Black Power revolutions and before 'black is beautiful' had set in. Naipaul complains of the self-contempt induced by slavery and colonial education; he cannot understand the obsession with whiteness; he is hostile to the mimicry that had spread even to the Indians; he cannot understand why Africans continue to feel guilty about their blackness and their Africanity; and he is appalled by the Africans' ignorance of Africa which for them was not a continent of darkness but an arena of shame:

Twenty million Africans made the middle passage, and scarcely an African name remains in the New World. Until the other day, African tribesmen on the screen excited derisive West Indian laughter; the darkie comic (whose values were the values of the Christian-Hellenic tradition) was more admired. In pursuit of the Christian-Hellenic tradition, which some might see as a paraphrase for whiteness, the past has to be denied, the self-despised (*The Middle Passage* p. 67).

Marcus Garvey knew what Naipaul was talking about. He it was who uttered the words that Bob Marley turned into a redemption song: 'We are going to emancipate ourselves from mental slavery because whilst others might free the body, none but ourselves can free the mind...' Naipaul's analysis of the situation of descendants of Africans in Trinidad are an encouragement to work at freedom from mental slavery. There is no sign of hating Africans in all of that. But turbulence arrives.

The awakening that Naipaul encouraged in *The Middle Passage* was happening on island after island as he travelled to research the book, and he began to be afraid of what he was seeing. He saw these stirrings as disordered, lacking in rationality and likely to get out of control. There was a paraphernalia of rebirth – slogans and symbols, loudspeakers and rallies, the beating of drums. Did he panic? There were roughly equal numbers of Africans and Indians in Trinidad. Would a West Indies-wide confederation of Africans with political control over an Indian minority come into being? I don't know if these were Naipaul's thoughts but the chapter on Trinidad ends ominously:

I came to see that such eruptions were widespread, and represented feelings coming to the surface in Negro communities throughout the Caribbean: confused feelings, without direction; the Negro's rejection of the guilt he has borne so long; the last delayed Spartacan revolt, more radical than Toussaint

73

L'Ouverture's; the closing of accounts this side of the middle passage (ibid p. 85).

Some would see not the ethnic panic but a contemptuous tone. The fear never left Naipaul and it got stronger – stopping just short of open hysteria.

It does not impress Naipaul very much that certain attitudes shared between Africans and Indians speak of some accord between the races. Trinidadians from the two ethnic groups shared tastes in relation to food and to consumer items in the stores. Sadly, both groups are on the weary road to whiteness and competing for white approval. 'But Trinidad, in fact, teeters on the brink of racial war. Politics must be blamed; but there must have been an original antipathy for the politicians to work on' (ibid p. 80). It is not known if anybody picked up on 'an original antipathy' about which, incidentally, Naipaul says no more in *The Middle Passage.* The problem of recognising difference and working for social and political unity at the same time had come to him as a troubling subject.

An African-Indian political party that came to power in British Guiana in the early 1950s quickly split along racial lines, and then there were killings. With knowledge of the racial atrocities of Guyana's politics fresh in his mind, Naipaul wrote *The Mimic Men* (1967), a penetrating account of the failure of African-Indian politics in a country called Isabella (Trinidad in thin disguise). This novel explores all the awkward questions that have to be asked and answered at every level in the society if attempts at African-Indian political unity are not to end in the calamity of racial war. The novel is a courageous examination of the obstacles to political unity between the two races. Naipaul cares enough for Trinidad to want political unity. In this novel, too, Naipaul allows Ralph Singh to voice the worst fears of an Indian living in Trinidad:

> I belonged to a small community which in this part of the world was doomed. We were an intermediate race, the genes passive, capable of disappearing in two generations into any of the three races of men, with perhaps only a shape of eye or flexibility of slender wrist to speak of our intrusion (*The Mimic Men* p. 57, Penguin edition).

This is probably an anxiety that Naipaul shares with his fictional character.

The fear that drives the severe analysis of Trinidad society in *The Middle Passage* and elsewhere is not one fear but a tangled cluster of fears –

including fear of racial annihilation, fear of the extinction of the writer and the existential fear of death. Naipaul's accounts of three visits to Trinidad from London allow us to see the continuity of a critical attitude ('hate') to the behaviours of the people of the island and a consequential resorting to the landscape from which he fled in 1950. To put it dramatically, he pulls out of the actual landscape an alternative landscape, a country of the mind which at once sustains him and binds him to the original on which it is based.

An old fear, old personal pain

The first of the journeys back took place in 1956: he had finished his studies and he had two novels awaiting publication. The account appears in *The Enigma of Arrival* (1987 pp 148-151).

> The steamship made landfall in Barbados: Seeing the 'flat hot worn-out looking land, the narrow streets, the insubstantial houses and little children everywhere' was like 'seeing very clearly an aspect of myself, and a past I thought I had outlived. The smallness of that past, the shame of that smallness...'.

After a morning tour, he was glad to return to the safety (his word) of the steamship which, leaving Barbados next morning, set him down on his own island where 'everything, had shrunk to Barbados size', and he found himself looking 'less at a landscape than at old personal pain'. In the first sentence of *The Middle Passage* account of the second return journey in 1960, a similar recoil is registered:

> As soon as the Francisco Bobadilla had touched the quay, the ship's side against rubber bumpers, I began to feel my old fear of Trinidad. I did not want to stay. I had left the security of the ship and had no assurance that I would ever leave the island again.

(Interestingly, he is like the traveller in the Chirico painting of which Naipaul was to make thematic use many years later.)

Trinidad was menacing: 'The world I thought I had left behind was waiting for me. It had shrunk, and I felt I had shrunk with it.' We are told here that 'the old fear' or the old personal pain 'waiting for me', had apparently begun to be felt in childhood. He was twelve-years-old when he set down in writing his vow to leave the island within five years. Naipaul's fear of Trinidad is first of all fear of the power to hurt that lay in the social and political ills the writer targets in the book. The old personal pain refers to something else. A clue might lie in *A House for Mr. Biswas*, a novel he tussled with during the four years after the 1956 visit to Trinidad.

The first return: glory dead

For most of the year before the original departure in 1950, young Naipaul lived in nervous fear that somehow he would lose the scholarship that was to take him to England and Oxford which, he states, was 'not a wish so much to go to Oxford as a wish to get out of Trinidad and see the great world and make myself a writer' (op cit 115) The abstract studies to which he had been subjected all his life and the conditioning of the Mother Country about what was literature and what kind of person a writer was had been converted into 'an idea of a literary life in another country' leading to more and more withdrawal from Trinidad and the ties that bind: 'My real life, my literary life was to be elsewhere.' In 1950, 'the excitement of departure' and the long journey to famous places, everything was tinged with the promise and the fantasies of the writing career and the metropolitan life. England was the first country of his mind.

Importantly, life in the extended family was a source of pain. When, to his embarrassment, members of the family converged on Piarco airport in 1950 to see him off, they could not have known what was going on in his head. Perhaps even he did not know where the phrase 'my real life, my literary life' would take him. It had not taken long for the colonially self-created myth of a glorious literary life in England to die. England was now simply a place where he could make a modest living while trying to write. In 1956 Trinidad, his father was dead, the family was in straitened circumstances and he had no money. He returned to the uncertainty of England in winter on a banana boat from Jamaica with 'an ache in my heart at my own insecurity...'.

The ache of the past

The four years after his return to England led to his release from the twice re-awakened personal pain that was the Trinidad of his early life:

> In those four years, out of the panic of that winter return to England, I had pulled much work out of myself, had written a book which I felt to be important (*Enigma* p. 151).

It was more the ghosts of the visit to Trinidad in 1956 than the stress of return to wintry England that harrowed him. The book he pulled out of himself was *A House for Mr. Biswas.* In the long course of the writing of this book, he tussled with his life in the Lion House, Chaguanas, and the transfer of much of it to the Capildeo houses in the city of Port of Spain; and he travelled over the beleaguered life of his father Seepersad Naipaul – the battles, the enthusiasms, the depression, the nervous breakdown and the anxious, life-long dream of being a writer. Near the end of the novel, disturbing memories, and the long gestation of someone's early years are alluded to, until we come to this settlement: 'So later, and very slowly, in securer times of different stresses, when the memories had lost the power to hurt with pain or joy, they would fall into place and give back the past' (Chapter 7, Part Two).

Freedom

My thesis is that the writing of *A House for Mr. Biswas* freed Naipaul to develop a new relationship to the natural landscape of his birth. The fear of Trinidad remained. He says in *Enigma* that the human landscape had been 'the landscape of anxiety, even panic, and sacrifice'. As a child he had never felt free. His education had been a race 'in which the fear of failure was like the fear of extinction'. Although A House for Mr. Biswas was still to be published, he was confident in 1960 that with that book he had made himself a writer and could live as a writer. Hence, the visit to Trinidad (September 1960 to May 1961) was tinged with celebration. The island had fed his panic and his ambition and it nurtured his fantasies, but in 1960 he was confident enough to visit the scenes of early trauma, moving from place to place 'to touch it with my mood of celebration, to remove from it the terror I had felt in these places for various reasons at different times' (*Enigma* p. 152).

But at this moment of seeming fulfillment, Naipaul begins to sketch out a new disposition. Though he had come 'to the end of a particular kind of fear', he says, his relationship with the island was at an end; his interest in it could be 'satisfied, even sated' in a day. He makes a distinction between the little island and its people who could no longer hold him; and on the other hand there was the British island of Muslims, Hindus and Africans that had given him, though he did not know it at the time, the great themes of displacement and the migration of peoples in the second half of the twentieth century. This side of the island eventually awakened in him a curiosity about the worlds of all the people who had come to it, worlds he recognised more and more as the worlds that had made him. The island put the whole world at the tip of his pen, sent him on journeys to all his connections, and made him more metropolitan than he had ever dreamed possible in that deluded time when London was his home. (*Enigma* p. 153).

The second element in the new disposition is the description of a two-fold landscape. He didn't need to say it, but he said that the Trinidad landscape the writer had created while living in England was not as accurate or full as he had pretended it to be. But the act of creation made him cherish the original. By the time we come to *The Loss of El Dorado* (1969), fabrication wins. Naipaul makes you feel that the Trinidad he created or discovered is more real than the degraded version in which he lived.

Country of the mind

In his account of the writing of *The Loss of El Dorado* (*Enigma* pp 155-160), Naipaul describes a scholarly process that unearths suppressed facts in the island's history and pre-history and, at the same time, outlines a sustaining country of the mind. Through the documents, he makes himself feel the antiquity of his island, its global character and the continuity of its hidden and fractured life: the undiscovered country joined to Venezuela and South America by the Orinoco whose floods mingled with the Atlantic; the primordial landscape of the First Peoples; the connections through Columbus with medieval Europe and the Spanish Empire; the fantasies and the frenzy of European adventurers, the coming of Africa and the East. And the sagas of men with grand ambitions and huge flaws, chasing a dream and coming to grief. The narrating character thinks that this book is the book he was destined to write:

> Ever since I had begun to identify my subjects I had hoped to arrive, in a book, at a synthesis of the worlds and cultures that had made me. … I felt in this history I had made such a synthesis (*Enigma* p. 157).

It is possible that it was what he learnt and imagined about Trinidad in the writing of *The Loss of El Dorado* that led Naipaul to understand the hidden depths of his growing dissatisfaction with living in England. It is significant that it was while finishing the 'history' of Trinidad that he decided to put 'an end to my time in England' (*Enigma* p. 157). It was Trinidad that finally broke the hold that England had over him. The attempt to live in Canada was quickly aborted. The attempt to leave England failed. The man who wrote *The Loss of El Dorado* might have thought of trying to live in Trinidad, but the requirements of the writer came first. To avoid extinction, the writer in him had to go back to England. The man was convinced at last that his departure from his island in 1950, with all it implied in homelessness and drift and longing, was final.

Later, he would escape to Wiltshire and learn a love for the landscape and geography of rural county. That is a fiction to be examined elsewhere. For now, our subject is *The Loss of El Dorado* and how it reflects his attitudes to Trinidad, and for that we must turn to the visit to the island in 1968-1969. It lies between what was going to be the final departure from England and other journeys accepting a freedom to move unencumbered from perch to perch, to be a roamer, to live the hotel life, to be free to say goodbye (*Enigma* p. 158).

The visit is in the nature of a farewell to the islands and it extends from Trinidad to St Kitts, Anguilla, Guatemala City and Belize City. He went first to his own island.

> I wanted to see the island where I had been living in a new way in my imagination for the last two years, the island I had restored, as it were , to the globe and for which I felt a deep romance (*Enigma* p. 158).

On this visit, the wilful translation of the Trinidad landscape into a landscape existing in his head is completed. He saw 'an island full of racial tensions and close to revolution', with an angry wish 'to destroy a world judged corrupt and too full of pain', a wish 'to turn one's back on it rather than to improve it'. Hate for 'the people and the anger that was like madness' is kept in check as he strives to see the landscape he had created in his imagination. He is determined to see the landscape he had created and to look for its aboriginal, pre-Columbus identity. 'The landscape of the past existed only in fragments. To see one such fragment, I looked at the drying-up mangrove swamp- green thick leaves, black roots, black mud' and 'From the top of Laventille Hill, among the shacks, I could imagine myself at the beginning of things if I looked selectively down the Gulf of Paria – grey, leaden, never blue- and the islets in the gulf' (*Enigma* p.160). Although he finds that this past existed only in fragments, he will not surrender the romance of the island that his research had divined.

On this visit, the narrating character sets above what is visible to common sight, the landscape he had brought into being in his writings: 'I had given myself a past, and a romance of the past. One of the loose ends in my mind had vanished; a little chasm filled. And though something like Haitian anarchy seemed to threaten my little island, and though physically I no longer belonged to the place, yet the romance by which I had attached it to the rest of the world continued to be possessed by me as much as the imaginative worlds of my other fictional books' (*Enigma* p. 164).

The hard-headed Naipaul's use of the word 'romance' does not manage to trivialise an attitude to the island that James Joyce had to his country when he said: 'When I die Dublin will be written in my heart.'

James Joyce wrote only about his Ireland. Naipaul wrote about Trinidad and out of Trinidad even when the setting of a work was not Trinidad. Trinidad was the truth that kept interrupting the effort to belong elsewhere that Naipaul made in *The Enigma of Arrival*. He feared and therefore hated the social, cultural and political pressures in island society and family life that threatened the writer with extinction. Like all would-be reformers, he met resistance and the hate of those who did not understand his underlying purpose. He turned inwards for justification and could claim with Joyce: 'Welcome, O life! I go to encounter for the millionth time the reality of experience, and to forge in the smithy of my soul the uncreated conscience of my race.'

It might be difficult to ever convince those who hate him as being anti-Trinidad that he wrote out of a love for the island of his birth, wrote to help it achieve the self-knowledge that would set it free. Thomas Aquinas knew that V. S. Naipaul needed someone who understood: 'Nothing is hated, save through being contrary to a suitable thing which is loved. And hence it is that every hatred is caused by love.' The country of the mind is the model of the 'suitable thing' that Naipaul loved.

The author dedicates this chapter to Tony Deyal, 'whose sense of the topsy-turvy world worries me and makes me smile'.

Note on the contributor

Kenneth Ramchand is Professor Emeritus of West Indian Literature, University of the West Indies, and Professor Emeritus of English, Colgate University, NY. He also served as President of the University of Trinidad and Tobago where, as Associate Provost, he established that university's

Academy for Arts, Letters, Culture and Public Affairs. Kenneth Ramchand (b. 1939) was educated at Naparima College, San Fernando, and the University of Edinburgh where he began his career as Lecturer in English in 1964. He is married to Averil, and his children are Gillian and Michael. He authored the pioneeering work, *The West Indian Novel and its Background*, and numerous other publications. He was a literary-cultural columnist in *The Trinidad Guardian* and served for more than ten years as an Independent Senator in the Government of Trinidad and Tobago. He loves fishing, and plays padder tennis with anyone who can move around a court.

Chapter 9

The great, frustrating, hilarious Trinidadian showed what we can be in the world

'Find your centre' was the advice he gave us all, says Kirk Meighoo who regarded Naipaul as his personal guide and mentor.

V. S. Naipaul's passing is being announced around the world, not always with fondness. He would have had it no other way, of course. He despised sentimentality and thoroughly enjoyed getting under someone's skin. He would do it on purpose just to get a laugh. 'Chooking fire', as it were. It was a very Trinidadian characteristic of his. One of many.

Paul Theroux noted scores of others in his wonderful, affectionate, broken-hearted memoir. Naipaul would often burst out singing a calypso in the most unlikely times and places – because he so enjoyed their politically incorrect, insightful wit and humour. His Queen's English, in speech and in writing, also had a Trinidad *bis* – or emphatic repetition. And, of course, he spoke about Trinidad often. It was the basis of everything he wrote. He himself stated that he only travelled to the places that were relevant to his experience growing up in Trinidad – Africa, the Islamic world, India, Britain, South America, the southern (plantation) United States. He refused invitations to visit and write about Eastern Europe and elsewhere for that reason.

Indeed, there is no person who has written more on Trinidad, for a longer period of time, to a wider audience than V. S. Naipaul. Even when he was writing about a country such as Malaysia, he would centre himself by noting: 'I recognised these trees from Trinidad when I was growing up.' This is not someone who hated himself or his heritage. He wrote extremely affectionately, with great detail, precision and care, but never flinching from the truth of his observations as he saw them. Indeed, more than anything else, he hated people who lied to themselves and, worse, banked on others believing those lies.

While Naipaul is wrongly criticised for not taking Trinidad seriously, the official statement of the Prime Minister of Trinidad and Tobago on Naipaul's passing proudly references his 1990 knighthood and his 2001 Nobel Prize, but nowhere mentions his 1989 Trinity Cross, the country's own highest honour. In contrast, Naipaul would later favourably comment that he received his Trinidad and Tobago award first, for which he did actually return to accept.

Often misunderstood

He was often misunderstood. For instance, the famous line, 'Nothing was created in the West Indies' was not a criticism primarily about the former slaves and indentures. It was a criticism of the British. He wrote that line in 1960 when we were still colonies. How could it mean anything else? In Spanish America, the colonialists built substantial public buildings, plazas and great universities that still stand today. In colonial New England, the venerable institutions of Harvard and Yale were built. Under British colonialism in the West Indies, massive wealth was generated here for a time, but nothing was created. They had no plans or ambitions for the region. We were what Naipaul's contemporary, Lloyd Best, called 'colonies of exploitation'.

From this background Naipaul had one obsessive concern: 'How do I, as a Trinidad Indian, born in this small colony, isolated from the rest of the world, marginal even here, find my way in the world?' It was the great theme of his life's work. He developed many sub-themes and recurring characters from it, returning to them over and over again: the futility of people trying to run away from themselves, the fraudulence and danger of white liberals, the Trinidad 'smart man' (a culturally specific form of con man, very pervasive) and the more brutal manifestations of this archetype in other societies. In fact, it is as if Naipaul spent his life writing just one Big Book, with each new publication simply being an additional volume or chapter in it.

When I put this to him, at our first meeting, he did not object. He paused. He accepted it.

That was not merely a piece of intellectual, literary, critical discussion, however. It was profoundly personal. It was the same personal question that I had learned from him to ask myself. But I had the gift of Naipaul exploring this issue publicly, in writing, for 50 years. It helped and guided me incalculably, as a Trinidad Indian outside of Trinidad, also travelling from country to country in my early years. He was my personal guide and mentor, in so many ways. The advice his father gave to him while he was abroad is what he gave to all of us: 'Find your centre.' It is the only then you can find your Way in the World.

That is why that meeting with him was surreal in so many ways.

After years of intense devotion to him and his work – my own PhD. thesis and first book was built on exploring and taking seriously Naipaul's profound idea of the 'half-made society' – one day, at home, I received a phone call.

> 'Hello, Kirk?' It was the low, calm, mellifluous voice I knew, but could not believe was on the other end.
>
> 'Hello?'
>
> 'This is Naipaul. I'm in Trinidad and I'd like you to come over for dinner.'

I couldn't believe it. But in some strange way, I knew that I would meet him one day. It seemed inevitable and I was waiting for it. The desire was too intense and persistent not to manifest. Of course, I went. I would change nothing about that evening. It was perfect. He personally confirmed everything I ever thought about him and his work.

This was one of the many times Naipaul visited Trinidad. He always did so quietly. While he was away, he used to ask his older sister, Kamla, to send him newspaper clippings. As source material, Naipaul always said that 'this land was pure gold … pure gold'.

That afternoon he had a small medical emergency procedure at Medical Associates in St. Joseph, a small town about 30 minutes away, which caused him to be late for dinner. He was thoroughly impressed and couldn't stop talking about it. 'I received better care there than I ever would in the UK,' he said. He was taken aback at how much Trinidad had progressed since the time he lived here.

I was surprised, and I qualified his statement, telling him how the concerns he raised almost 50 years earlier and continued to elaborate were equally valid today. He disagreed, and told me stories about the one local doctor whom everyone had to go to when he was a child, and whom he considered to be a 'quack'. It was a surreal moment, with Naipaul defending Trinidad and I criticising it! We laughed a lot that evening. He was hilarious and constantly made dry, sharp jokes.

How absurd Trinidad humour pervades his even bleakest books

In fact, many critics of Naipaul don't realise how much absurd Trinidad humour pervades even his bleakest work. When an interviewer in the 1970s asked him why he no longer wrote comic works, he disagreed.

> 'You can't be serious,' she queried.

> 'I am,' he said.

> 'Surely, *Guerillas* [his novel of 1975], for example, can't be considered humorous.'

> 'You should hear me read it.'

And it is absolutely true. Naipaul shares the wicked, contrarian humour of so many classic calypsos which he loved, or the everyday, absurdist, politically incorrect hilarity of Trinidad, which is why I would title my own analysis of his work, Sans Humanité: *The Perverse, Trinidadian Worldview of V. S. Naipaul.* (*Sans humanité* is a phrase associated with extempore Trinidadian calypso duels, in which opponents trade insults in entertaining, clever, often merciless ways.)

If one were offended by his remarks, then be doubly aware: he would push as many of your buttons as he could perceive, just to have fun watching you lose your mind. The book of his collected interviews is uproarious just for that alone.

I always appreciate the Trinidadians who maintained their deep appreciation of him in the 1970s in particular, while he was writing some of his most difficult work, charting a new course not pursued by anyone else in the world, and before he was so universally acclaimed.

Many do not realise the importance that the Trinidadian intellectuals Eric Williams (the renowned historian and country's first prime minister) and the Marxist C. L. R. James (all three of whom attended Trinidad's Queen's Royal College) had on this phase of Naipaul's life. Naipaul himself attests to this. He credits James with making him realise the larger, universal themes and issues that were unconsciously underpinning *A House for Mr. Biswas*, and they corresponded. (Naipaul reciprocally admired James's cricket memoir, *Beyond a Boundary,* published around the same time as *Biswas*).

In 1960, Eric Williams – as Premier of Trinidad and Tobago in the now-forgotten Federation of the West Indies – invited Naipaul to travel to the Caribbean and write his first book of non-fiction, which became *The Middle Passage*. Williams gave Naipaul use of his substantial personal library. On the other hand, Prime Minister A. N. R. Robinson later told Naipaul that it was because he read *Among the Believers* that he was able to understand and deal with the Jamaat-al-Muslimeen as he was held hostage during the failed 1990 coup.

In my own view, every Trinidadian must read three of Naipaul's works: the Trinidad chapter in *The Middle Passage* (1962), 'Michael X and the Black Power Killings in Trinidad' or *The Killings in Trinidad* (1980), and for an extended meditation on the Trinidad 'smart man', *A Way in the World* (1994). There are no more profound analyses of who we are as a people.

I genuinely, deeply love V. S. Naipaul. He helped me immeasurably. And he showed all of us what we can be on the world stage. I take this opportunity again to thank him for the life he lived and shared.

Note on the contributor

Kirk Meighoo is the author of *Politics in a 'Half-Made Society': Trinidad and Tobago, 1925-2001*, in part a tribute to V. S. Naipaul. He is a multi-media personality, public speaker, former University lecturer, and has served as an Independent Senator in Trinidad and Tobago and on various government committees. He is a friend of the Naipaul family in Trinidad.

The first version of this article was published at:
http://www.icdn.today/post/v.s.-naipaul-the-great-frustrating-hilarious-trinidadian-showed-what-we-can-be-in-the-world.

Chapter 10

Scientist as well as artist

Lloyd Best argues in this essay written in 2001 after V. S. Naipaul was awarded the Nobel Prize for literature, that his unique vision rejects ideological impositions and, instead, is founded in scientific observation.

I am surprised Frank Abdulah, the Tobago diplomat, recalls Vidia Naipaul at Queen's Royal College (QRC), Port of Spain, as a student who simply came and went. My recollection of him is as a celebrity, even then.

I have a clear picture of my first encounter, sometime in 1945. It was during the last minutes before the mid-day resumption. I'd sneaked upstairs from Third to Sixth Form. Not the done thing. Ours was the class of 1946. It inhabited a room on the ground floor, in the main block, under the clock. If you exited by East North East, you were on your way. Once up, pass the den to your left where the specialists in Maths, Phys, Chem performed their sundry mysteries. To the right lay the home of the Humanities. Latin, French, and Spanish were not always on their own as a scholarship specialisation. Students had also to distinguish themselves in English Language, Literature and History, European and English. In that year, the famous name was William Demas, then waiting to go off to Cambridge and passing time teaching French downstairs to the likes of Denis Solomon, Reggie Dumas, John Neehall and the rest of us. That lunch break, for some reason, it seemed especially animated in heaven. It was the first time I'd ever tiptoed up, promptly to be chased. But there I'd glimpsed him on the balcony, in khaki shorts, Cambridge blue shirt, standing and holding court. It is the image that lasts.

I recall an evening in 1960. Naipaul was on tour to write what became *The Middle Passage*. He'd been invited to lecture at the students' union, Mona. He arrived on the hour. The rest of us operated Jamaica time. Refusing to indulge us, he folded his tents. 'Please take me away.' We returned to 38

College Common. A huge crowd soon turned up in my drawing room to hear him. He held court, as only he could.

As if my luck would last, I was thrice lucky, in Port of Spain, later that year. Lloyd Braithwaite and I were a team on mission to help William Demas, then director of the Economic Planning Division of the Office of the Prime Minister of Trinidad and Tobago, with the Second Five-Year Plan. Seven months we lived in government quarters in Petit Valley, newly built, on the right going up, just before Simeon Road and Sparrow's Hideaway. It was as if God had planned a regal. For dinner, he cast Trinidad's three finest raconteurs. My wife cooked a corker. Along with Braithwaite were James and Naipaul, all with wives.

In the company, it was hard for Naipaul to hold court but he did. I felt twice blest. I'd paid no admission fee. And yet, I cannot say I've ever got to know him, save through his oeuvre. We crossed once or twice in London, at the BBC. Possibly in the mid-1970s, I stumbled upon him in the campus of the University of the West Indies at St. Augustine. In the twilight, he was walking with his family, just where the old train line ran south. We exchanged greetings, chatted for perhaps 15 minutes.

The penetration, the insight, the industry, the craft – and the sparkle

I'm happy he's at last got the prize that puts matters right. You might be sceptical of his human posture. No doubt about the penetration, the insight, the industry and the craft. And the sparkle, holding court. Had he not been selected for the Nobel, he'd have been no less compelling a figure. But as one of us, I'm not so sure he did not need the validation that the prize has given. With that I have no quarrel. More than anyone else, he has taught us the reasons why West Indians so crave such tribute. Many think Paul Theroux's *Sir Vidia's Shadow* (1998) was an exposure, if not an assassination. I find it simply lifts the masks Naipaul has worn the better to play himself, like any other Trinidadian. I'm happy for his family and the rest of us, more assured now that he's legitimate. I congratulate Naipaul. He has created an effective context for work and that's what is important.

His magnum opus is, of course, A *House for Mr. Biswas* (1961). The metaphor is powerful for a people like us, needing a native tradition and a past. Naipaul is so distressed by our loss, he considers himself homeless. In his work, the real characters are the dislocated and the terrified. He has become fascinated with Islam. Worse than colonialism, he thinks, it has blocked out the memory of converts. Perhaps only to the Arabs has it conceded dignity or ancestry.

The Caribbean predicament is not very different. Particularly the educated know little about country, culture or self. The work that has detained my attention most is *The Suffrage of Elvira* (1958). It is not the most subtle or elegant. The narrative skill was only just in the making. It is a little contrived. It is in the remarkable powers of observation and scrutiny, now his trademark, that lies Naipaul's appeal. The novelist was 18. It was the second election on the basis of adult suffrage. First time round in 1946; he was 14. But he'd discerned that the Trinidad and Tobago public had not 'seen the possibilities'.

His theme is familiar: government from above with little politics from below. Elections were then, and are still largely now, mostly business opportunities. Make money by any means. This is society, not lawless, but with no concept of law or responsibility. Were not our peoples transplanted only to lose old tradition while finding new tradition almost impossible to create? Is the problem not identity? Is it not the terror of being, with little reference to time or to place?

The mis-match between culture and institutions

It is precisely Naipaul's point that we suffer a mis-match between culture and institutions. The irony may be that, if such a condition were truly understood, it would carry real possibilities for an order free of monarchy, oligarchy or class. Does the promise of the Caribbean not lie in a Creole ethos, still to be forged from the sensibilities of slaves and indentured workers? Might that not be the main chance for democracy and participation?

Naipaul is clearly pessimistic. He has not yet seen that some of us are still driven by that vision. For all his insight, he probably does not yet realise that the first act to create such as order is to paint the picture exactly as it is. His own contribution is that he has refused romance. He does not pretend we're anything we pretend to be. In *Elvira*, he was the first to describe the fractures as they are. Only incidentally and not exclusively, are they racial. Bonding is indeed primal. We're so panicked, only the most convenient basis, the most automatic, the most mindless, would do. In that sense, solidarity is frankly ethnic.

In *Elvira*, the parties are Spanish, Hindu, Muslim, Negro. In Naipaul's clinical way, they invoke all of religion, colour, class, language and homeland as well as race. To grapple with complexity, the treatment is simple. Naipaul adds to our self-knowledge. He rejects ideological impositions. The political sociology he devises is founded in scientific observation. The hardware of our constitution may sound like Westminster but the software of our political culture makes a government and politics of its own kind. Novelist and writer that he is and artist supreme, craftsman of the prose, it is the scientist in him which, at this precise moment, has come to the fore.

Note on the contributor

Lloyd Best (1934-2007) was a Trinidadian intellectual, columnist, professor and economist. This chapter was first published in the *Trinidad and Tobago Review*, Vol. 23, Nos 9-10

Chapter 11

'The sense of historical wonder never left him'

The need to confront the past unflinchingly was central to Naipaul's work and worldview, argues Bridget Brereton.

Many people much better qualified than me have written, or will write, about V. S. Naipaul's wonderful literary achievements. I want to think about his sense of history.

The need to understand the past, to confront personal, national and regional histories unflinchingly, seems to me to be absolutely central to Naipaul's work and worldview. For him, the erasure of the past, the failure or refusal to develop well researched and reasonably objective historical narratives were key indices of underdevelopment and intellectual impoverishment for any people, nation or region of the world.

A society which cannot or will not examine its past with scholarly rigour was, in his view, a society doomed to be static and uncreative. It was a society which substituted tradition, barely understood rituals, and fundamentalisms of various kinds, for a critical examination of its history. Naipaul knew this examination was difficult and painful, but he believed it would open up the possibility of creativity and development. Speaking at a conference at St Augustine in 1975, he said:

I think it is through scholarship and a wish to understand through scholarship, and not through sentiment, that we can arrive at some understanding of all the strands in our upbringing. ... I think that through scholarship and intelligent enquiry we will understand more about the past and more about the culture of our grandfathers than they themselves did.

In his own journey to self-knowledge, Naipaul often said the years he spent researching *The Loss of El Dorado* (1969), his only full-length work of formal 'history', were enormously important in helping him to locate his place in the world. He returned again and again to the source materials he studied in the British Museum and the old Public Records Office, in London, for that book. (He told my late colleague, Keith Laurence, that this archival research was the hardest work he had ever done.) In his Nobel Lecture (2001), Naipaul described almost as a personal epiphany his discovery, sitting in the British Museum in 1967 reading old Spanish documents, that his birthplace Chaguanas was named after a small Amerindian ethnic group, the Chaguanes, mentioned in a letter from the King of Spain in 1625: 'And the thought came to me in the museum that I was the first person since 1625 to whom that letter had a real meaning. ... We [the Capildeo clan] lived on the Chaguanes' land.'

His arduous work on the archives, he wrote in 1984, 'trying only to understand how my corner of the New World ... had become the place it was', endowed him with a sense of 'historical wonder' which never left him, and which he clearly believed was essential for intellectual and social development.

In *The Enigma of Arrival* (1987), Naipaul described his two years in the archives as 'a great packed education'. Coming from an island and a community which then had little interest in its past, where 'history' happened only in other places, he was energised by a new understanding of his place-and therefore his way-in the world. 'I was amazed, reading the documents of my island in London, by the antiquity of the place to which I belonged. ... Seeing the island as part of the globe, seeing it sharing in the antiquity of the earth! Yet these simple things came to me as revelations.'

'My island', 'the place to which I belonged': whatever Naipaul may have written or said (or failed to say) about Trinidad, especially when he was being deliberately mischievous, no one should doubt that he was, indeed, created right here. Or that he believed the work of historical research was central to understanding his island and its complexities, as it was for every place on earth.

Note on the contributor

Bridget Brereton is Professor Emerita of History at the University of the West Indies, St Augustine, Trinidad. This tribute first appeared at https://www.trinidadexpress.com.

Section 3

His complex and contradictory literary legacy

Richard Lance Keeble

V. S. Naipaul has a standing in the literary world like none other. On the one hand he is celebrated as a genius, he wins the Booker Prize and the ultimate accolade, the Nobel Prize for literature. For many writers he has proved an inspiration: significantly, he drew up a list of seven rules for beginner writers at the request of the Indian news magazine, *Tehelka*:

1. Do not write long sentences. A sentence should not have more than ten or twelve words.
2. Each sentence should make a clear statement. It should add to the statement that went before. A good paragraph is a series of clear, linked statements.
3. Do not use big words. If your computer tells you that your average word is more than five letters long, there is something wrong. The use of small words compels you to think about what you are writing. Even difficult ideas can be broken down into small words.
4. Never use words whose meaning you are not sure of. If you break this rule you should look for other work.
5. The beginner should avoid using adjectives, except those of colour, size and number. Use as few adverbs as possible.
6. Avoid the abstract. Always go for the concrete.
7. Every day, for six months at least, practise writing in this way. Small words; short, clear, concrete sentences. It may be awkward, but it's training you in the use of language. It may even be getting rid of the bad language habits you picked up at the university. You may

go beyond these rules after you have thoroughly understood and mastered them.

But on the other hand, Naipaul is reviled – even demonised. In *The Booker Prize and the Legacy of Empire*, Luke Strongman sums up these criticisms, commenting: 'Naipaul's writing is constrained by its rigidity, an unwillingness to consider what are seen as the positive aspects of cultures in conditions of flux and change, and also by the way he depicts the bathos of the post-colonial encounter without a counterbalancing positivity or affection' (2002: 64).

In this section, there is an attempt to capture those two very different kinds of responses. According to Nicholas Laughlin, who has edited a revised and expanded edition of Naipaul's early family correspondence, Sir Vidia was 'the most Trinidadian writer Trinidad has produced, in all good and bad ways'. While *A House for Mr. Biswas* (1961) 'remains the closest thing we have to a Great Trinidadian Novel', *The Loss of El Dorado* (1969) is 'still the most bracing and penetrating history of colonial Trinidad'. Laughlin concludes:

His lifelong subject was how the unfeeling forces of history — especially the huge movements of peoples between and within cultures, driven by the colonial enterprise — play out in the lives of ordinary people. He was fascinated by the making and remaking of the individual demanded by these dislocations. His family, the island of his birth, the far-flung places he travelled to, and his own misunderstandings and illusions were equally apt for scrutiny.

Ameena Gafoor argues that Naipaul did not care what people thought of him; he was a man with a mission even if he was accused of transferring his own neuroses onto his characters. The stories in *The Mystic Masseur* (1957), in particular, 'made us realise that ordinary people were the characters in fiction, that the purpose of fiction is to hold up a mirror to the society (and many of us did not like what we saw in the mirror)'.

Diana Athill, OBE, the celebrated literary editor, novelist and memoirist, was his publisher when *In a Free State* won the Booker Prize in 1971. She has mixed memories of Naipaul as a novelist – and as a man. She remembers him as 'easily the most difficult writer' she had ever worked with. At the same time, she admired him enormously: he'd set out to be a writer and he had done it. 'He must have had an instinct for it, but it was very deliberate. And, of course, I always liked his work but I began to dislike him more and more as a person because of how he was about his wife, Pat. She might not have existed.'

For Jug Suraiya, the prominent Indian journalist, author and columnist, one of Naipaul's greatest works was *The Mimic Men* (1967) in which he had lampooned the manners the 'brown sahibs' of post-Independence India had borrowed from their erstwhile British rulers. Yet, in the end, according to Suraiya, Naipaul himself is perhaps best seen as a product of post-colonial mimicry. In effect, he was a 'nowhere man': caught between the three worlds of Trinidad, a long-lost India and an uneasily adopted England.

In that he was the mimic man supreme, he was the embodiment of Sartre's description of genius as 'the scandalous audacity of nothingness'.

Reference

Strongman, Luke (2002) *The Booker Prize and the Legacy of Empire*, Amsterdam and New York: Edition Rodopi

Chapter 12

His world was what it was: the enigma of V. S. Naipaul

Always at the heart of his writing was the quest for self-understanding, argues Nicholas Laughlin.

He was the rare literary figure of sufficient notoriety that newspapers had kept draft obituaries on file for decades. When news broke on 11 August 2018 that V. S. Naipaul had died at the age of 85, press coverage was swift and voluminous. It was a front-page story in Trinidad and Tobago's three daily newspapers, the Nobel laureate's photograph blown up above the headlines.

On the social networks where most of T&T's public debate now unfolds, some commentators pounced on the detail that the international press described Naipaul as a British writer. 'He would have loved that,' was a typical response. For those who disapprove of Naipaul—and he courted disapproval—one longstanding grouse was his supposed disavowal of Trinidad, the island where he was born and grew up. We remember the sting of Naipaul's statement on receiving the 2001 Nobel Prize: 'It is a great tribute to both England, my home, and to India, the home of my ancestors, and to the dedication and support of my agent.' Full stop. So, to be eulogised as British: surely that was his wish all along?

But the facts are complicated. Born in a British colony, Naipaul was a British subject when he left Trinidad in 1950, 18-years-old, on a hard-won scholarship to Oxford. He was permanently settled in London by the time Trinidad and Tobago became an independent nation in 1962. He was 'British' all along, and at the same time he never really belonged in his adopted country. The evidence is plain to read in his books.

Naipaul was 'Trinidadian to the core,' says Kenneth Ramchand, the eminent literary scholar. 'Trinidad made him. It shaped him, and even when he was vexed with Trinidad, it haunted him throughout his career.' I'd go further and say Naipaul was the most Trinidadian writer Trinidad has produced, in all good and bad ways. *A House for Mr. Biswas* remains the closest thing we have to a Great Trinidadian Novel with its unsentimental portrait of an Indo-Trinidadian family striving for a sense of coherence and self-determination in a small society 'at once exceedingly simple and exceedingly confused'. *The Suffrage of Elvira* (1957) is the most valuable primer for anyone trying to understand T&T's incorrigibly tribal politics (according to no lesser authority than the political theorist Lloyd Best). *The Loss of El Dorado* (1969) is still the most bracing and penetrating history of colonial Trinidad. And the picaresque stories of *Miguel Street* (1959), his breakthrough book, have more pervasively influenced subsequent Trinidadian fiction writers than any other text.

Naipaul always portrayed his writing as a quest for self-understanding: 'I had to do the books I did because there were no books about those subjects to give me what I wanted.' And 'those subjects' are the historical circumstances into which he was born, in the Trinidad of 1932. In the essay 'Prologue to an Autobiography', he offered a summary:

> ... there was a migration from India to be considered, a migration within the British empire. There was my Hindu family, with its fading memories of India; there was India itself. And there was Trinidad, with its past of slavery, its mixed population, its racial antagonisms and its changing political life; once part of Venezuela and the Spanish empire; now English-speaking, with the American base and open-air cinema. ... And there was my own presence in England, writing. ... So step-by-step, book by book ... I eased myself into knowledge.

'I am the sum of my books'

'I am the sum of my books,' he said. And the self he created in his books was deliberately free of loyalties to anything but writing itself. He strove to achieve 'a freedom from people, from entanglements, from rivalries, from competition'. He added: 'One doesn't have a side, doesn't have a country, doesn't have a community; one is entirely an individual.' This stance put Naipaul in conflict with many other Caribbean writers and, indeed, with many Caribbean readers.

For decades, Caribbean literature has been animated by unresolved arguments about responsibility, language, authenticity — about how to be a Caribbean writer. Naipaul remained aloof from these debates. The relatively good-humoured satire of his early fiction set in Trinidad matured in the 1960s into a sharper, more pessimistic criticism of what Naipaul saw as the pretensions of post-independence Caribbean societies – 'half-made', inhabited by 'mimic men'. As he travelled more widely, he extended his scrutiny to other postcolonial nations in Asia, Africa and South America. Nowhere did he pull his punches. He was accused of exaggerating the squalor of India, of hostility to Islam. His descriptions of black Caribbean people and Africans often seem to betray racial anxiety, if not outright prejudice.

And in a spirit of serious mischief, he baited his critics with outrageous remarks. In a profile published soon after Naipaul won the Nobel Prize, my colleague Jeremy Taylor listed some memorable slurs:

> Over the years, he has called people monkeys, *infies* (inferiors), bow and arrow men, potato eaters, Mr. Woggy. He has described whole countries as 'bush'. Oxford University, where he earned his degree in English, was 'a very second-rate provincial university'. Africa 'has no future' and as for African literature 'you can't beat a novel out of drums'. He once recommended that Britain should sell knighthoods through the Post Office (this was before he became Sir Vidia Naipaul).

His merciless banter – perfected by Trinidad's calypsonians

Trinidadians ought to recognise these provocations as his version of our very own picong, the mocking, merciless banter perfected by our calypsonians. We should understand his impish public conduct as Naipaul 'playing himself' as Trinidadians describe the performance of a carefully crafted persona that at once masks and reveals. His biographer Patrick French quotes the Barbadian writer George Lamming's suggestion that Naipaul was 'playing ole mas' — 'masquerading or making trouble for his own entertainment, a Trinidadian trait'. French adds: 'When he was being rude or provocative in this way, Naipaul was full of glee.' This is the irony that exposed the man behind the writer: he was never more Trinidadian than when he was bad-talking Trinidad.

And so the most thoughtful responses to his death have also been the most conflicted. No one can come away from French's biography, *The World Is What It Is*, without feeling repulsed by Naipaul's bigotries, his misogyny, his cruelties aimed at loved ones and strangers alike. But then there are his books, written in prose of beautiful rigour and clarity, their relentless probings sometimes finding an unexpected tenderness.

His lifelong subject was how the unfeeling forces of history — especially the huge movements of peoples between and within cultures, driven by the colonial enterprise — play out in the lives of ordinary people. He was fascinated by the making and remaking of the individual demanded by these dislocations. His family, the island of his birth, the far-flung places he travelled to, and his own misunderstandings and illusions were equally apt for scrutiny. And his books, at their best, give us portraits of our societies and ourselves which we can't deny, even when we'd prefer to. There are books of Naipaul's I hope never to read again, and books of his without which I can't understand the world I was born into.

'Everything of value about me is in my books.' That may be the truest sentence Naipaul wrote. It's not a question of whether the work justifies the sins of the man. That is too simple an equation. The power and, yes, the beauty of his writing is in some way the product of the writer's flaws, and also in some way transcends those flaws, without absolving them. The moral algebra of art is difficult, and it should trouble us. There is no better example than the books of V. S. Naipaul. It is one of the reasons—the great reason—I feel compelled to read him.

Note on the contributor

Nicholas Laughlin edited a revised and expanded edition of V. S. Naipaul's early family correspondence, *Letters Between a Father and Son* (2009). This piece was first published at https://globalvoices.org/2018/08/12/his-world-was-what-it-was-the-enigma-of-v-s-naipaul/.

Chapter 13

The philosopher – and creator of timeless characters

Naipaul did not care what people thought of him; he was a man with a mission even if he was accused of transferring his own neuroses onto his characters, argues Ameena Gafoor.

Naipaul was perhaps the most controversial contemporary literary figure, vilified and criticised as a man, but as a writer he drew unparalleled admiration from the world of literature.

Naipaul not only wrote in a lucid, unambiguous style but he playfully exposed men and women for their falsities. V. S. was just 18 years when he entered Oxford University in 1950. By 1957, he had published *The Mystic Masseur* which lovingly poked fun at the Trinidad he grew up in and remembered from every angle but which also exposed false gods, portraying characters who were mimics and who had no sense of identity. His characters, like G. R. Muir, M.B.E., are emblematic of the wider society.

We, in fact, came to that delightful book of short stories, simply titled *Miguel Street* (1959), which went on to win the Somerset Maugham Award, before we came to *The Mystic Masseur* (actually published two years earlier), and those stories made us realise that ordinary people were the characters in fiction, that the purpose of fiction is to hold up a mirror to the society (and many of us did not like what we saw in the mirror). Characters such as Hat, Bolo, Man-Man, B. Wordsworth, Bogart and the unforgettable Laura became immortal for us. Those characters are timeless.

Novel after novel by V. S. Naipaul revealed the dilemma of being a colonial, the complex matters of dispossession, placelessness, and identity, the emptiness of the post-colonial world, the quest for self-knowledge and freedom. Among the fictional works Naipaul wrote are *The Suffrage of*

Elvira (1958); *A House for Mr. Biswas* (1961); *The Mimic Men* (1967, and winner of the W. H. Smith Award); *In a Free State* (1971; Booker Prize); *A Bend in the River* (1979) and *The Enigma of Arrival* (1987).

Naipaul embarked on travel in 1960 and produced writings too many to list in this tribute. In one of them, *Finding the Centre* (1984) is a perceptive discussion of his emergence as a writer. His travel writings were a way of challenging the imperialist form of the novel that we had inherited, of finding another form to question man and society. V. S. Naipaul even ventured into the Muslim world in his pursuit of truth and said things which angered Muslims. He angered Africans, women, and West Indians by saying: 'History is built around achievement and creation; and nothing was created in the West Indies....', but Naipaul did not care what people thought of him; he was a man with a mission even if he was accused of transferring his own neuroses onto his characters. A writer does not need philosophical training to write; he is the philosopher.

Naipaul richly deserved the Nobel Prize (2001) and the Honour of Knighthood bestowed by Queen Elizabeth 11 in 1990. In 2007, on a visit to Trinidad, he appeared on a public platform, and a few of us from Guyana (including Bernadette Persaud, Ryhaan Shah and myself) travelled to Trinidad with the hope of catching a glimpse of the man who had done us all proud. At question time, a man from the audience ventured a question whereupon, Naipaul, as gentle as a lamb, like a father to a four-year-old child, replied: 'Can you find another question? You asked me that one already.' That is the writer who people vilified as being 'strange' and 'cold'.

Giving us a clear sense of who we are

At that meeting, I presented the writer with copies of *The Arts Journal*. I doubt he gave them a second glance and I don't fault him for that because I appreciate that he spent his life educating us, giving us a clear sense of who we are as post-colonial West Indians from diverse ancestral roots, and our place in the scheme of things.

V. S.'s younger brother, Shiva, was also a prolific writer whose *Fireflies* (1970; winner of three awards including the John Llewellyn Rhys Memorial Prize, the Jock Campbell *New Statesman* Award, and the Winifred Holtby Memorial Prize) and *The Chip-Chip Gatherers* (1973; Whitbread literary Award) are also profound statements on the complicated questions of culture and the place of Indians in Trinidad. Shiva died in 1985 aged just forty but not before he had written four more works: *North of South* (1978);

Black and White (1980); *A Hot Country* (1983); and *Beyond the Dragon's Mouth* (1984).

In fact, it was their father, Seepersad Naipaul, a journalist, who was first bitten by the writing bug; he read the classics including Shakespeare and Dickens to them; by example, he led the family into a scalding awareness of the post-colonial world. His *Gurudeva and Other Stories* was ultimately published (1976) by André Deutsch long after his death. Now, the news has it that their sister Savi has just released a book about her brother. Perhaps in her book we will discover the reason her brother, so critical of the imperialist world, chose to spend most of his life in England. Trinidad and the English-speaking Caribbean owe much to this family and Hanuman House has a place in history.

The Arts Journal records its condolences to family and admirers. V. S.'s passing has left a lamentable void; it may well be decades before the West Indies produces a writer as fearless as Naipaul to tell us bluntly about ourselves.

Note on the contributor

Ameena Gafoor is Editor of *The Arts Journal*, author of *Aftermath of Empire: The Novels of Roy A. K. Heath* (UWI Press, 2017) and recipient of two national awards (Guyana) for work in the arts and culture of Guyana and the Caribbean.

Chapter 14

'He was easily the most difficult writer I've ever worked with'

Diana Athill, V. S. Naipaul's first publisher, remembers a brilliant, difficult man – and the books that made his name.

I remember the night Vidia won the Booker Prize for *In a Free State* in 1971. He'd always behave as if things like this were a bore, and he said he wouldn't go. I very rarely scolded him, but at this point I said: 'You will bloody well come. How can we go on publishing you if you won't collaborate?' He behaved reasonably well. He didn't walk out, which he often did. I don't think he ever thanked anyone for anything, but he rather grudgingly went up and got his cheque.

By that stage I was working very hard at keeping affection for him. I'd liked him very much when he was young because he was so clever and funny. I remember our first meeting in a coffee shop in Soho, near my office. He was this little, very shy person and I was delighted by his stories. Francis Wyndham loved them too, but André Deutsch was doubtful – he wondered who was going to buy these stories about someone talking in a Trinidadian way about things that nobody in England cared about.

André said he had to write a novel first and if that was successful we'd publish the stories. Fortunately he was just finishing his first novel. *The Mystic Masseur* was quickly followed by *The Suffrage of Elvira*. But the stories – *Miguel Street*, published in 1959 – are very good and they add up to a wonderful picture of Trinidad.

I admired him enormously. What was wonderful was that he'd made himself – he'd set out to be a writer and he had done it. He must have had an instinct for it, but it was very deliberate. And, of course, I always liked his work but I began to dislike him more and more as a person because of how he was about his wife, Pat. She might not have existed. She once said to me: 'Vidia doesn't like me coming to parties because I'm so boring.' She went on being his wife even when he'd been with Margaret, his Argentinian lover, for a long time. He, foolish man, had never read Pat's diaries and handed them over to his biographer, Patrick French, saying write as you find, which Patrick bravely did. There was a lot in those diaries that was very chilling.

I'd never disliked anything in his books until *Guerrillas*, in 1975. It was based on people I knew and he'd got the woman completely wrong. I said he might perhaps rethink things and he went quite still and then said: 'I'm sorry, I did the best I could' and walked out of the room. I thought, now what? 'Now what' was his agent ringing to say he was leaving. He came back, but Vidia and I were much more business-like after that. We never had lunch together or talked about anything except the books.

The first time he left, I remember saying to André: 'It's such a relief I don't have to make myself like him any more.' André roared with laughter and I realised he felt just the same. He was so moody and depressive. You only had to look at his face to see that he was genuinely suffering a lot of the time.

The end of our publishing relationship was quite sober. I stopped caring and it was much easier. He was easily the most difficult writer I've ever worked with. After we stopped working together I never saw him again. His last wife would say: 'Oh you must come and see him,' but I never did. When I heard he'd won the Nobel Prize in 2001 I was very pleased. I think I sent him a congratulatory letter. You don't have to be a good person to be a good writer.

He was never our biggest selling writer. We hung on to him because in those days we could afford to, if we admired someone's writing. If it was today, I doubt he would have had a career like that, because publishers can't support writers who don't sell. Those were nicer days. And the wonderful thing is that *A House for Mr. Biswas* – which I think is his greatest novel – has never been out of print

Note on the contributor

This article first appeared in the *Guardian* at
https://www.theguardian.com/books/2018/aug/17/diana-athill-vs-naipaul-delighted-stories.

Chapter 15

The mimic man supreme

Perhaps no one has put the enigma of exile under more accomplished literary scrutiny than V. S. Naipaul, writes Jug Suraiya.

A three times exile himself, V. S. Naipaul exemplified the saying that the only true homeland of the writer is his own imagination.

Naipaul was born in Trinidad to parents brought from India as labourers. That was his first exile. He recalled his mother telling him: 'Leave India to the Indians.' Nor could Trinidad's insular horizon accommodate his questing mind. He went to Britain, to study on a scholarship, and even though he lived there for the rest of his life, he never seemed quite at home there either. As he wrote, he always felt he was in 'another man's space'.

In his writings, sharp as a surgeon's scalpel, he courted controversy. As elsewhere, in India he was both idolised and demonised. His two early books on India, *An Area of Darkness* (1964) and *India: A Wounded Civilization* (1977), provoked the wrath of the left as well as the right for showing the poverty, squalor and corruption of a caste-riven society.

However, after the 1992 demolition of the Babri Masjid – which he approved of – in the city of Ayodhya, Uttar Pradesh, and the rise of Hindutva, the ideology which seeks to establish the hegemony of the Hindu way of life, which he described as the result of a '700-year-old sense of revenge' against Mughal rule, Naipaul became the darling of the Hindu Right, and the bane of the Muslim intelligentsia.

In *The Mimic Men* (1967), he had scathingly lampooned the mores and manners that the 'brown sahibs' of post-Independence India had borrowed from their erstwhile British rulers. Though he never used the term himself, he would have applauded the pejorative of 'Macaulayputras' bestowed on them by proponents of Hindutva.

However, with his penetrating social and cultural X-ray vision, Naipaul himself could not have seen himself as being other than a similar product of post-colonial mimicry, a nowhere man who — caught in a limbo between three worlds, of Trinidad, a long-lost India and an uneasily adopted England — had to invent and find himself in a language he stole with unsurpassed skill from those responsible for shaping his post-colonial destiny.

In that he was the mimic man supreme, he was the embodiment of Sartre's description of genius as 'the scandalous audacity of nothingness'.

Note on the contributor

Jug Suraiya is a prominent Indian journalist, author and columnist. This article first appeared at https://blogs.timesofindia.indiatimes.com/jugglebandhi/vs-naipaul-nowhere-man/.

Section 4

Provocation was an essential part of his personality

Richard Lance Keeble

As many commentators stress, V. S. Naipaul was essentially a contrarian. He revelled in the humour of the classic calypsos he loved and in the everyday, politically incorrect hilarity of his home country, Trinidad. He deliberately set out to ruffle feathers, and if you were offended – then that was your problem.

Urvashi Bahuguna, blogger at *scroll.in*, sets the scene for this section on Naipaul the provocateur, listing some 13 times he 'stirred the pot of controversy with objectionable statements'. These range from his comment during an interview in 2011 that he didn't consider any women writer his match and his assertion at another time that Islam had destroyed India ('The intellectual life of India, the Sanskrit culture, stops at 1000AD. Islam was the greatest calamity that befell it.') to his claim that 'Africa has no future.'

According to Orlando Patterson, a Jamaican-born American sociologist and novelist known for his work regarding the history of slavery and freedom as well as race and development, V. S. Naipaul was a great novelist but an outright racist. The fact that he was dark-complexioned and self-loathing made his prejudices no less vicious and no more excusable. Patterson suggests that Naipaul could never forgive himself for his blackness and the misfortune of being a close descendant of low caste 'coolies' – possibly the main reason for his mental breakdown at Oxford University. 'I remain thoroughly disgusted by his lifelong airing of his contempt for Trinidad, the West Indian home that nurtured his distinctive genius, whose black and Indian taxpayers paid for his education' is Patterson's stark conclusion.

Narissa Deokarran, who blogs at *loveoflogic.com*, is, in contrast, deliberately measured in her critique. She is particularly critical of his attitudes to women. The many cruelties he inflicted on those closest to him were starkly revealed, she says, in the authorised biography written by Patrick French. Lady Patricia, his first wife, 'probably suffered the most'. While she was in remission from cancer and had just undergone a mastectomy, she 'learnt that her husband had been sleeping with prostitutes for years through a magazine article!' Naipaul even described himself as a 'great prostitute man'. But Deokarran also encourages us to see and understand the whole man with all his contradictions:

He was a complex person with sides that were not so 'great' but nevertheless should be acknowledged by his admirers as being part of the man. Almost every famous and influential person in the world has attributes that are inconsistent with what made them stand out and be worshipped by thousands if not millions.

Finally in this section, the great American maverick intellectual Edward Said didn't mince his words in his critique of Naipaul, published in *Al-Ahram Weekly*, in 1998. He contends that, somewhere along the way, Naipaul suffered a serious intellectual accident. His obsession with Islam caused him somehow to stop thinking, to become, instead, a kind of mental suicide compelled to repeat the same formula over and over. Naipaul's 400-page critique of Islam, *Beyond Belief*, he condemns, arguing that it is:

> ... based on nothing more than this rather idiotic and insulting theory. The question isn't whether it is true or not but how could a man of such intelligence and gifts as V. S. Naipaul write so stupid and so boring a book, full of story after story illustrating the same primitive, rudimentary, unsatisfactory and reductive thesis: that most Muslims are converts and must suffer the same fate wherever they are.

Chapter 16

Thirteen times Naipaul stirred the pot of controversy with objectionable statements

From Islamophobia to misogyny, the Nobel laureate expressed problematic thoughts many times over. By Urvashi Bahuguna.

This is a list that captures some of the damage Naipaul caused in his lifetime to the world's perception of subjects including Africa, Islam, his homelands – India and Trinidad – and women writers.

1. Naipaul said in an interview in 2011 that he didn't consider any women writer his match. He dismissed Jane Austen as 'sentimental'. He said women had a 'narrow view of the world' because 'inevitably for a woman, she is not a complete master of a house, so that comes over in her writing too'.

2. In an authorised biography by Patrick French, it was disclosed that Naipaul berated his wife if she overcooked the fish and told her she did not behave like the wife of a writer, cheated on her and expected sympathy for the guilt he felt, and hit the woman he had an affair with to the point where she couldn't appear in public for some time.

3. He thought very poorly of the Trinidadian people. In one remark of many, he said: 'I can't see a Monkey – you can use a capital M, that's an affectionate word for the generality – reading my work. … These people live purely physical lives, which I find contemptible. … It makes them only interesting to chaps in universities who want to do compassionate studies about brutes.' In another, he described Trinidad as 'unimportant, uncreative, cynical, a dot on the map'.

4. He wrote about ex-colonies such as India and Trinidad but for Western audiences. 'I do not write for Indians,' he said in a 1998 interview, 'who in any case do not read. My work is only possible in a liberal, civilised Western country. It is not possible in primitive societies.'

5. Explaining to the same interviewer what a *bindi* or a 'red dot' on the forehead of millions of Indian women signified, he said: 'The dot means: my head is empty.'

6. Naipaul believed that 'Africa has no future'. Of Africans, he wrote: 'It was hard to arrive at a human understanding of the pigmies, to see them as individuals. Perhaps they weren't.'

7. He argued that 'there is a certain "scum" quality in Latin America'.

8. Naipaul compared the effects of Islam to the effects of colonialism, and decided that the former had been worse for the world. He claimed that Islam 'has had a calamitous effect on converted peoples. To be converted you have to destroy your past, destroy your history. You have to stamp on it, you have to say: "My ancestral culture does not exist, it doesn't matter."' He went even further to say: 'Islam destroyed India. ... The intellectual life of India, the Sanskrit culture, stops at 1000AD. Islam was the greatest calamity that befell it.'

9. Naipaul said 'no reconciliation' was possible between Islam and other religions on the subcontinent because Islam 'is a religion of fixed laws. This goes contrary to everything in modern India'.

10. He defended the unlawful demolition of Babri Masjid by Hindu nationalists as 'inevitable retribution' and saw in it a 'passion' and 'new, historical awakening.' He told Khushwant Singh, Indian author, journalist, lawyer, diplomat and politician, that it was 'an act of historical balancing'.

11. He thought that the Hindu gangsters he had been brought to meet in Mumbai were Muslim because 'As a community they somehow seem to be historically more drawn towards crime than all the others.' When corrected, he asked the gang leader leading questions about the Muslims in the gang.

12. About religious intolerance, he wrote: 'I think people who are not sexually fulfilled are hard people and extraordinarily damaged. They are terribly unhappy and unreliable. Lots of sexual repression comes out in the form of violence. A lot of religious intolerance is a product of sexual frustration.'

13. He impatiently criticised Shashi Deshpande and Nayantara Sehgal, two award-winning Indian novelists, for discussing how gender affects their writing. His habit of interrupting and insulting women at literary events has been well-documented.

Note on the contributor

Urvashi Bahuguna blogs at *scroll.in*. This is an edited version of an article which first appeared at https://scroll.in/article/890932/thirteen-times-vs-naipaul-stirred-the-pot-of-controversy-with-objectionable-statements.

Chapter 17

How he out-Trumped Trump on Africans and West Indians

V. S. Naipaul was a genius as a novelist but an outright racist and the fact that he was dark-complexioned and self-loathing made his prejudices no less vicious and no more excusable, according to Orlando Patterson.

In the sixties, when I lived in London, it was common knowledge among fellow West Indian students that V. S. Naipaul would move to the other side of the road with an expression of utter disgust if he saw any of us approaching. Indeed, the things he wrote about Africans and West Indians, and later Indians, out-Trumped Trump.

Another matter: critics seem to carry their admiration for his novels over to his non-fiction writing, which is ridiculous. These writings are in the tradition of elegantly expressed 19th century pre-social science personal effusions with little regard for accuracy or representativeness. His *The Middle Passage* (1982) travel book on the West Indies is superficial – influenced mainly by the 19th century racist James Anthony Froude's, *The English in the West Indies* (1888).

It always amazes me that none of the many non-Caribbean literary critics who write about his fiction note the single most important source of his distinctive style – his Trinidadian cultural background. Trinidad is invariably mentioned as the land of his birth, and little else, with emphasis on his exile and tortured relation with Britain, as if his parents had him there unexpectedly on a tourist visit.

In fact, Naipaul's greatest gift, his incomparable irony and cunning wit, is thoroughly Trinidadian. You hear Naipaul at every turn, and in every conversation among Trinidadians who are notorious among West Indians for their cutting humour and devastating sarcasm, especially when they mercilessly tease each other in the practice known as 'picong' or pretend to flatter others by the wicked verbal play known as 'mamaguy'. You don't have to take my word for it: just engage a taxi driver in conversation on the way from the airport in Port-au-Spain.

In his early years in Britain Naipaul was known to have one of his sisters write frequently to him about street life in Trinidad. And speaking of his sister, I was hardly surprised to learn that his three surviving sisters in Trinidad had not been invited to his funeral according to the British *Telegraph*. After all, he never held a funeral for his first, horribly treated, British wife.

I can pity and sociologically understand his self-hatred, the fact that he could never forgive himself for his blackness and the misfortune of being a close descendant of low caste 'coolies' —quite possibly the main reason for his mental breakdown at Oxford where, at eighteen, he suddenly found himself surrounded by people whose whiteness he so desperately envied and, as the quintessential colonial, somewhat feared-- but I remain thoroughly disgusted by his lifelong airing of his contempt for Trinidad, the West Indian home that nurtured his distinctive genius, whose black and Indian taxpayers paid for his education.

Note on the contributor

Professor Orlando Patterson, of Harvard University, is a Jamaican-born American sociologist and novelist known for his work regarding the history of slavery and freedom as well as race and development. His book, *Freedom, Volume One: Freedom in the Making of Western Culture* (1991), won the US National Book Award for Nonfiction.

Chapter 18

Reflecting on the good and the bad of the man

Narissa Deokarran argues that V. S. Naipaul was a cold, narcissistic and emotionally dead person – and particularly cruel towards women.

A literary giant has died and the Caribbean mourns. V. S. Naipaul, the Nobel laureate, recipient of a knighthood from Queen Elizabeth II and son of the Caribbean soil, was immensely admired for his great prose. But who was the man behind the books? Was he revered among those closest to him and did he treat them with the kindness that the public expects from one bestowed with such gifts?

One needs to be exceptional to have that 'extra special something' to gain thousands of admirers. To win the Nobel Prize for literature and receive a knighthood is for many the pinnacle of international recognition.

With regard to Naipaul's treatment of women – especially those closest to him – there was nothing 'great' and worthy of emulating. Many cruelties were laid bare in his authorised biography by Patrick French, *The World Is What It Is* (2008). Naipaul's brutal frankness and disregard for the feelings of his women were boldly illustrated. Nothing was deemed too embarrassing, he just didn't care because it was all about painting an authentic image and not a fakery of half-truths and honeyed characterisation to make him appear a saint in the eyes of the public.

Naipaul told his biographer that the more he abused his mistress, Margaret Gooding with whom he spent 24 years, the more she wanted it. He lamented that on one occasion his hand was hurting badly after beating Ms Gooding and her face was too damaged to be shown in public. He even said that she didn't 'mind' the abuse. This elicited the only reaction from her to his biography. She simply said that she had 'minded'. Naipaul even crudely spoke about their sex life after dumping her for a new woman. The many episodes with his women are too numerous to list here but can be read about in his biography and the articles from leading outlets online.

Lady Patricia, whom he met while he was at Oxford University, was his first wife and companion for over 40 years. She was the one who probably suffered the most from his cruelty. She was aware of the other woman because her husband insultingly discussed his escapades and feelings for his mistress with her. From what is revealed she was a broken and beaten figure from years of abuse by Naipaul and apparently had no say in what he did. In one of her diary entries she wrote: 'Vidia told me he had not enjoyed making love to me since 1967.' She was merely the cook, cleaner and editor of the great man's books. Summing up the impact of his affair on his wife, he said: 'I was liberated. She was destroyed. It was inevitable.' Then he claimed that Lady Patricia accepted the situation and his own sister, Savi, was forced to rebuke him harshly.

Naipaul described himself as 'a great prostitute man'

Even before the biography was published, while she was in remission from cancer and had just undergone a mastectomy, Lady Patricia learnt that her husband had been sleeping with prostitutes for years through a magazine article! Naipaul described himself as a 'great prostitute man' and proudly related his exploits to the magazine knowing that it would make headlines around the world and not caring that his wife was sick and about how it would affect her. Talk about the greatness of the man.

Naipaul was such a cold, narcissistic and emotionally dead person that he was unable to empathise and care about those he tortured with his acts and words. The life that Lady Patricia had with the great V. S. Naipaul reads like a chilling tale of the horrors of a victim with her abuser, certainly not an enviable position. Even while she lay dying from cancer in 1996 he was courting the future Lady Naipaul. He did not spare his dying wife the details of his new conquest. The event of her death failed to provoke feelings of remorse, guilt or compassion in Naipaul. In fact, Lady Nadira moved into the house a day after the cremation.

Apart from cruelties which Naipaul visited upon his women who were in awe of him, he harboured an inherent dislike of and belief in the inferiority of women generally. Statements issued from his own mouth over the decades confirmed this and even in his elderly years he remained steadfastly unapologetic about his misogynistic utterances. Sadly, the women who remained by his side and held him he destroyed and the ones who admired from afar were dismissed as unworthy by his generalised sexist statements. Naipaul was a giant in the literary world and is an icon for many established and upcoming writers but can he ever be associated with female empowerment and promotion of women's rights?

The man was a Jekyll and Hyde sort of person. Although many women admired him and wrote glowing tributes over the years he famously put them to shame by stating he considered no female writer his equal in an interview at the Royal Geographic Society in 2011! Then to put the cherry on top, he pronounced that 'a woman is not a complete master of her house and so that comes across in her writing'. When asked for a comment on these pronouncements, the Writers' Guild of Great Britain said it would not 'waste its breath on them'. A very fitting reply for a misogynistic, narcissistic literary genius.

Even Jane Austen on the chopping block

The international icon, Jane Austen, was even put on the chopping block. Naipaul dismissed her writing as sentimental, a quality considered by him as frivolous and feminine. Then Indian women writers were criticised for their 'banality' when writing on British colonialism. While his points are arguable, egomania no matter the 'greatness' of the source is never an endearing quality in either men or women.

Although, Naipaul's parents were of Indian descent and he never spoke poorly publicly of his mother the reasons behind his contempt for women remain a mystery. He famously said that the red dot worn on the forehead of Indian women means 'my head is empty'. He was admired for his frankness and honesty yet his many outbursts on women were just ravings without legitimate reasons. He criticised women writers as not being his equal yet provided no proof. The red dot on the forehead of Indian women means that they are married. Naipaul of course, knew this as he grew up among people of Indian descent yet he chose to insult without reason.

Naipaul spent his entire life irking people with the full force of his brutal 'truths'; he revelled in the discomfort and provoked with all his might. Would he have wanted only fawning tributes? While Naipaul's undisputed greatness in the literary world was firmly cemented decades ago, he was a complex person with sides that were not so 'great' but nevertheless should be acknowledged by his admirers as being part of the man. Almost every famous and influential person in the world has attributes that are inconsistent with what made them stand out and be worshipped by thousands if not millions. Reflect on the good and the bad; the complete person, the greatness and the faults. It reflects that entire being like it should: we are all the same.

Note on the contributor

Narissa Deokarran is a teacher in Guyana who blogs at loveoflogic.com. This chapter is based on her letter which appeared at https://www.stabroeknews.com/2018/opinion/letters/08/22/reflect-on-the-good-and-the-bad

Chapter 19

An intellectual catastrophe

Somewhere along the way Naipaul suffered a serious intellectual accident. His obsession with Islam caused him somehow to stop thinking, to become, instead, a kind of mental suicide compelled to repeat the same formula over and over, according to Edward Said, in this 1998 assessment.

The originally Trinidadian but later British author V. S. Naipaul brought out a massive volume about his travels in four Islamic countries -- all of them non-Arab -- as a sequel to a book he wrote on the same four places about 18 years previously. The first book was called *Among the Believers: An Islamic Journey* (1981); the new one is *Beyond Belief: Islamic Excursions Among the Converted Peoples* (1998). In the meantime, Naipaul has become Sir V. S. Naipaul, an extremely famous and, it must be said, very talented writer whose novels and non-fiction (mostly travel books) have established his reputation as one of the truly celebrated, justly well-known figures in world literature today.

In Paris, for example, Sonia Rykiel's fancy showrooms on windows on the Boulevard St Germain are filled with copies of the French translation of *Beyond Belief*, intermixed with the scarves, belts and handbags. This, of course, is one kind of tribute, although Naipaul may not be very pleased about it. On the other hand, the book has been reviewed everywhere in the prestige English and American press, paid tribute to as the work of a great master of shrewd observation and telling detail, the kind of demystifying, thorough exposé of Islam for which Western readers seem to have a bottomless appetite. No one today would write a similar kind of book about Christianity or Judaism. Islam on the other hand is fair game, even though the expert may not know the languages or much about the subject.

Naipaul's, however, is a special case. He is neither a professional Orientalist nor a thrill seeker. He is a man of the Third World who sends back dispatches from the Third World to an implied audience of disenchanted Western liberals who can never hear bad enough things about all the Third World myths -- national liberation movements, revolutionary goals, the evils of colonialism -- which in Naipaul's opinion do nothing to explain the sorry state of African and Asian countries who are sinking under poverty, native impotence, badly learned, unabsorbed Western ideas like industrialisation and modernisation. These are people, Naipaul says in one of his books, who know how to use a telephone but can neither fix nor invent one.

Naipaul can now be cited as an exemplary figure from the Third World. Born in Trinidad he is originally of Hindu Indian stock; he emigrated to Britain in the l950s, has become a senior member of the British establishment and is always spoken of as a candidate for the Nobel Prize -- someone who can be relied on always to tell the truth about the Third World. Naipaul is 'free of any romantic moonshine about the moral claims of primitives' said one reviewer in l979, and he does this without 'a trace in him of Western condescension or nostalgia for colonialism'.

Naipaul and the 'Islam problem'

Still, even for Naipaul, Islam is worse than most other problems of the Third World. Feeling his Hindu origins, he recently has said that the worst calamity in India's history was the advent and later presence of Islam which disfigured the country's history. Unlike most writers he makes not one but two journeys to 'Islam' in order to confirm his deep antipathy to the religion, its people and its ideas. Ironically, *Beyond Belief* is dedicated to his Muslim wife Nadira whose ideas or feelings are not referred to. In the first book he does not learn anything -- they, the Muslims, prove what he already knows. Prove what? That the retreat to Islam is 'stupefaction'. In Malaysia, Naipaul is asked 'What is the purpose of your writing? Is it to tell people what it's all about?' He replies: 'Yes, I would say comprehension.' 'Is it not for money?' 'Yes. But the nature of the work is important.' Thus he travels among Muslims and writes about it, is well paid by his publisher and by the magazines that run extracts of his books, because it is important, not because he likes doing it. Muslims provide him with stories, which he records as instances of 'Islam'.

There is very little pleasure and only a very little affection recorded in these two books. In the earlier book, its funny moments are at the expense of Muslims, who are 'wogs' after all as seen by Naipaul's British and American readers, potential fanatics and terrorists, who cannot spell, be coherent, sound right to a worldly-wise, somewhat jaded judge from the West. Every time they show their Islamic weaknesses, Naipaul the Third World witness appears promptly. A Muslim lapse occurs, some resentment against the West is expressed by an Iranian, and then Naipaul explains that 'this is the confusion of a people of high medieval culture awakening to oil and money, a sense of power and violation and a knowledge of a great new encircling civilization [the West]. It was to be rejected; at the same time it was to be depended on'.

Remember that last sentence and a half, for it is Naipaul's thesis as well as the platform from which he addresses the world: The West is the world of knowledge, criticism, technical know-how and functioning institutions, Islam is its fearfully enraged and retarded dependent, awakening to a new, barely controllable power. The West provides Islam with good things from the outside, because 'the life that had come to Islam had not come from within'. Thus, the existence of one billion Muslims is summed up in a phrase and dismissed. Islam's flaw was at 'its origins -- the flaw that ran through Islamic history: to the political issues it raised it offered no political or practical solution. It offered only the faith. It offered only the Prophet, who would settle everything -- but who had ceased to exist. This political Islam was rage, anarchy.' All the examples Naipaul gives, all the people he speaks to tend to align themselves under the Islam vs the West opposition he is determined to find everywhere. It's all very tiresome and repetitious.

How Islam converts 'suffer the fate of the inauthentic'

Why then does he return to write an equally long and boring book two decades later? The only answer I can give is that he now thinks he has an important new insight about Islam. And that insight is if you are not an Arab -- Islam being a religion of the Arabs -- then you are a convert. As converts to Islam, Malaysians, Pakistanis, Iranians and Indonesians necessarily suffer the fate of the inauthentic. For them Islam is an acquired religion which cuts them off from their traditions, leaving them neither here nor there. What Naipaul attempts to document in his new book is the fate of the converted, people who have lost their own past but have gained little from their new religion except more confusion, more unhappiness, more (for the

Western reader) comic incompetence, all of it the result of conversion to Islam. This ridiculous argument would suggest by extension that only a native of Rome can be a good Roman Catholic; other Catholic Italians, Spaniards, Latin Americans, Filipinos who are converts are inauthentic and cut off from their traditions. According to Naipaul, then, Anglicans who are not British are only converts and they too, like the Malaysian or Iranian Muslim, are doomed to a life of imitation and incompetence since they are converts.

In effect, the 400-page *Beyond Belief* is based on nothing more than this rather idiotic and insulting theory. The question isn't whether it is true or not but how could a man of such intelligence and gifts as V. S. Naipaul write so stupid and so boring a book, full of story after story illustrating the same primitive, rudimentary, unsatisfactory and reductive thesis: that most Muslims are converts and must suffer the same fate wherever they are. Never mind history, politics, philosophy, geography: Muslims who are not Arabs are inauthentic converts, doomed to this wretched false destiny.

The pity of it is that so much is now lost on Naipaul. His writing has become repetitive and uninteresting. His gifts have been squandered. He can no longer make sense. He lives on his great reputation which has gulled his reviewers into thinking that they are still dealing with a great writer, whereas he has become a ghost. The greater pity is that Naipaul's latest book on Islam will be considered a major interpretation of a great religion, and more Muslims will suffer and be insulted. And the gap between them and the West will increase and deepen. No one will benefit except the publishers who will probably sell a lot of books, and Naipaul, who will make a lot of money.

Note on the contributor

Edward Said (1935-2003) was Professor of Literature at Columbia University and the founder of the discipline of post-colonial studies. © Copyright *Al-Ahram Weekly*. All rights reserved. Originally published in the issue dated 6-12 August 1998.

Section 5

Brief encounters: on the other sides of the man people met...

Richard Lance Keeble

Naipaul, the public man seemingly so harsh as he sounded off on women and Islam, and the other Naipaul, the friend, the mentor, even the gentle, cat-adoring, caring man are the subjects of this section.

Anil Dharker is a columnist and writer, and the Founder and Director of the Mumbai International Literary Festival which is held in November every year. Here, he shares his memories of times with the Great Man. Most recently, while Naipaul was touching eighty, frail and in a wheelchair, he appeared to Dharker to have willingly surrendered to the strong will of his second wife, Nadira, Lady Naipaul as she liked to call herself, a Pakistani journalist. On another occasion, during a festival stage conversation with his friend, the writer (and joint editor of this text) Farrukh Dhondy, Naipaul had revealed his emotional side:

When Dhondy spoke about *A House for Mr Biswas*, the book which made him famous and whose central character was based on his journalist father, there was no response. In the silence we noticed the tears running down Naipaul's cheeks. Later in the conversation there was yet another moment of emotional distress, strangely enough when Dhondy talked about the death of Sir Vidia's cat.

At the same time, he treated his critics 'with a silence bordering on disdain. V. S. Naipaul's books spoke for him, and that was that'.

Ahsan Akbar, who grew to be a friend after a chance encounter on the London Tube, says that the writer's warmth and softness have not been emphasised enough. He was one of those by Naipaul's hospital bed during his final days. Earlier, when Naipaul was already in a wheelchair, Akbar had accompanied him during an on-stage interview, which proved to be his last:

> I had been unaware of the titan's stage fright and his incredible shyness. When the announcements were being made, Sir Vidia held my hand gently as we waited backstage. His grip tightened as soon as we started moving. ... When the hour-long session ended, he asked if he was good enough.

Next, Colin Grant remembers vividly the time Naipaul visited the BBC's Bush House, to appear on the World Service programme he was producing. As they proceeded into the building, Sir Vidia held out his elegant fedora and gave it him to hold – as if he were his valet. Naipaul's writings on Trinidad had first deeply affected Grant: 'I recognised its source in the antipathy that kith can feel for kin; Naipaul was Trinidad's recalcitrant prodigal son, whose rejection of his homeland deeply hurt his compatriots and whose affection they most craved.' Then Grant saw the 'Brahmin's snobbery and defeated gloom of *India: A Wounded Civilization*' lifting to give way to 'the near celebratory *India: A Million Mutinies Now*'. All this was leading up to the (beautifully evoked) Joycean epiphany moment at Bush House.

When Naipaul reached for the fedora I did not let go of it immediately. In that moment I wanted him to know that despite all the writing of 'ill-made Negroes' I had remained in his corner. Here was the evidence: I had held his hat – and it was intact.

Chapter 20

How he treated his critics: with silence bordering on disdain

Anil Dharker shares some memories of his times with Naipaul – and reflects on his second marriage, personality and reputation.

I didn't know him well enough to call him Vidia, while Sir Vidia seemed far too formal, so I did what I imagine most people did: I didn't address him by any name at all.

He was coming home for dinner the first time I met him. We had invited a few friends, but word spread quickly, and soon a few became the many. (And everyone came on time). On the way to the house he had a request: could we stop by at Banganga? 'I have never been,' he said by way of apology. I didn't dare admit I hadn't been either. What would he have thought? Philistine, probably, for ignoring something so historic and right in the neighbourhood.

He seemed to know Banganga`s mythology: in the great epic *Ramayana*, Rama and his brother Lakshman stopped here on their journey to rescue Sita from Sri Lanka. Feeling thirsty, Lakshman pierced the ground with his arrow and water gushed out to form a pond (*Ban*: arrow, *Ganga*: from the river Ganga or Ganges).We had to walk a bit from the car, and I became acutely aware of the squalor around us. Various passages of *An Area of Darkness* came to mind, and I wondered if this would now figure in a future book, an excoriation of our treatment of our monuments, revered only in the rhetoric of 'our glorious past'.

He had walked briskly then; more than twenty years later and touching eighty, he was in a wheelchair, frail in body, subdued in speech. The latter may have had something to do with the presence of Nadira, Lady Naipaul as she liked to call herself, the Pakistani journalist he had married a few years earlier and who now seemed to have taken charge of his life. How much, one incident will make clear. He was in Mumbai to receive the Tata Literature Live! Lifetime Achievement award at our literary festival, and to get over jet lag had come in a couple of days earlier, so we had taken him out for a quiet dinner. 'What will you have?' I asked him. 'I think I will go vegetarian today,' he said. 'No,' Nadira's stern voice said commandingly, 'You will have fish.' Sir Vidia had fish.

It seemed to me then, and at a subsequent meeting the next day, that he had willingly surrendered to the strong will of his wife. I wanted to ask if being married to a Muslim from a theocratic state like Pakistan had changed his views on Islam, which were strong, and his critics contended, bigoted. But then, one doesn't ask these questions, does one? However, if you look at his bibliography, *Beyond Belief: Islamic Excursions Among the Converted Peoples* was published in 1998; most of his later work (except for *The Masque of Africa* in 2010) is personal in nature, a great writer looking back at his life, his views softened by age. Perhaps he had already said what he wanted to say about Islam, and Nadira came into his life as real life irony, the irony which so distinguished his writing.

At our awards ceremony he sat on the NCPA's Tata stage in conversation with his friend of many years, the writer (and joint editor of this text) Farrukh Dhondy. Naipaul was in his wheelchair, one leg stiffly and awkwardly askew which he seemed powerless to move. When Dhondy spoke about *A House for Mr Biswas*, the book which made him famous and whose central character was based on his journalist father, there was no response. In the silence we noticed the tears running down Naipaul's cheeks. Later in the conversation there was yet another moment of emotional distress, strangely enough when Dhondy talked about the death of Sir Vidia's cat. Do we all get emotional with age, even writers who are sharp of observation and even sharper of expression?

Five years later, what everyone remembers about the award is Girish Karnad's speech at our festival, when he turned what was to be a talk on theatre into a vitriolic attack on Naipaul for his 'rabid antipathy towards Indian Muslims'. Karnad's assault, for that's what it was, was based on a remark supposed to have been made by Naipaul on the demolition of Babri Majid: 'It was an act of passion. Any passion is to be encouraged. Passion leads to creativity.' Farrukh Dhondy, who was with Naipaul when these remarks are alleged to have been made, has always maintained that they were never made. If so, why didn't Naipaul deny them when they began to circulate, and nip the rumour in the bud? 'That's not his way,' his friends say. 'How did Vidia react to the Karnad attack?' I asked Nadira. 'He didn't react. He never reacts.'

So it is that allegations about Naipaul's misogyny, his racism, his Islamophobia, his contempt for his native Caribbean and all else that threatened his reputation as the finest writer of the English language, went unanswered. Sir Vidia wrote books; he wrote many, all crafted so brilliantly that you admired them even when occasionally being repelled by his views, and that's what he did. He treated his critics and his detractors with a silence bordering on disdain. V. S. Naipaul's books spoke for him, and that was that.

Note on the contributor

Anil Dharker is a columnist and writer. He is the Founder and Director of the Mumbai International Literary Festival which is held in November every year. He is also the Founder and Director of Literature Live! which holds literary evenings through the year. This tribute first appeared as https://timesofindia.indiatimes.com/vs-naipaul/vs-naipaul-a-visit-to-banganga-was-his-only-request/articleshow/65380346.cms?

Chapter 21

His gentle side

Ahsan Akbar, who grew to be a friend after a chance encounter on the London Tube, says that the writer's warmth and softness have not been emphasised enough.

When I went to see V. S. Naipaul in hospital he was feeling marginally better. His wife Nadira had arranged for a violinist to play some Mozart to him, helping him relax. She did not allow too many visitors. This was not the first time he had been in hospital. His health had been deteriorating for the past 12 months and the family had been receiving – as always – a flurry of invitations from literary festivals and heads of state. All had to be declined. In his hospital room we discussed his coming 86th birthday and I suggested that we celebrate with champagne at the Ritz. He smiled and proposed we go to 'the other place'. He had a better time at the Lanesborough and preferred to head there, instead. We both knew that his time with us was limited: perhaps weeks, or months if we were lucky.

In the end, it was only three days. His wife summoned a few close friends to his bedside. One was Geordie Greig, the new editor of the *Daily Mail*, who read Tennyson's 'Crossing the Bar' to him. I only held his hand. His body was not co-operating but his mind – a surprise for the doctor – was incredibly active. For me, there were too many memories. Thousands of images flashed in what seemed like a second; and it took me back to our first meeting, purely a chance encounter.

The first time I met the Naipauls was on a carriage of the London Underground. It was sheer luck that I should find myself sitting next to Sir Vidia on a Northern Line train. For an aspiring writer, trying to find my way in London, he was the great post-colonial writer to look up to, an absolute icon. I took my chances to tell him, as politely as possible, that I had finished reading *In a Free State* only the previous night. 'How interesting,' he said, and nodded. But he was not interested in my illuminating thoughts on the book.

In fact, he was never interested to hear what other people thought of his writing (critics very much included). Instead, he was curious about me, asking what I did for a living, and so on. 'Temping,' I said, as was the case with many of my peers who graduated in the aftermath of 9/11, hustling to secure a choice place in the City. He looked visibly pained, for he did not approve of the word: 'temporary work' would have been his choice of expression. Sir Vidia was punctilious about everything, from reading your facial structure to noting punctuality. If he did not like your face, there was little hope that he would see you again. But somehow I passed his tests — and two years ago, I took my chances again.

This time, I wanted him to travel 6,000 miles to Bangladesh. My two co-directors and I had this great wish for him to inaugurate the sixth Dhaka Literary Festival. Sir Vidia was in a wheelchair by then and it was a big ask for him to travel to this tiny country in a remote part of the world, but he immediately agreed. Several friends, including Paul Theroux, had told him it was unwise to go to such a dangerous location, but that did not stop him. There was only one condition: he wanted to see the birds which migrate there to escape the Siberian winter.

A writer cannot be afraid, he said on stage a few months later, to rounds of applause. I had been unaware of the titan's stage fright and his incredible shyness. When the announcements were being made, Sir Vidia held my hand gently as we waited backstage. His grip tightened as soon as we started moving. But it was also a hallmark of his sincerity that he did not want to let us down. When the hour-long session ended, he asked if he was good enough. It turned out to be his last public interview.

Sir Vidia enjoyed his fish but avoided meat, which made him a pescatarian – some of the obituaries have suggested he was a strict veggie. He was as fascinated by the world of business as he was by people's habits. He was curious and he liked to have fun with those he knew he could trust. He appreciated it if you dressed up for him, as he too would make an effort to present himself in the most impeccable manner.

I once remarked that he looked like a film star in one of the framed photographs that hung on his bedroom wall. He was immensely pleased. It was a great capture of him from the late 1970s, looking contemplative in a beautiful blazer, with the proof of *A Bend in the River* in front. 'Oh, would you please tell that to Nadira?' he said, and smiled.

Since his death, we have heard much about V. S. Naipaul, the author and personality. Condescending, heartless, misogynistic — all manner of terms have been bandied around, but they don't fit the man I knew and loved. His literary record is known worldwide, but I will remember him for his courage, warmth and softness, which were apparent to any of those lucky enough to have had the opportunity to know him.

Note on the contributor

Ahsan Akbar's collection of poems, *The Devil's Thumbprint*, is published by Bengal Lights Books. This article first appeared at https://www.spectator.co.uk/2018/08/v-s-naipauls-gentle-side/.

Chapter 22

When Sir Vidia held out his fedora – and gave it me to hold...

Colin Grant remembers the time Naipaul visited the BBC's Bush House – and how his simple act demonstrated that V. S. 'remained in his corner'.

A dozen years ago V. S. Naipaul strolled into the atrium of Bush House. He was to appear on the World Service programme that I produced. A small retinue fussed around him; he seemed amused and serene. We found him a seat and I knelt beside him and whispered that he was the writer I most admired; he had defined the world for me. Naipaul nodded more out of expectation than appreciation. After a while he stood and as we proceeded into the building Sir Vidia held out his elegant fedora and gave it to me to hold – as if I were his valet.

Thirty years earlier, Viv, a book-loving uncle, had introduced me to the exacting delight of Naipaul's writing; we championed him for demonstrating, through his literary virtuosity, that descendants of immigrants could be just as erudite and accomplished as the very best of our British hosts.

Like my Jamaican parents, Naipaul's formative years under colonial rule in Trinidad were a time when, as was often said, it was the ambition of every black and Asian man to be white. Even in the early comic work of *Miguel Street*, his colonial anxieties over class and race were exposed. He'd inherited the notion of writing as an honourable vocation from his father. With *A House for Mr. Biswas*, Naipaul made good on that investment: the novel was an act of filial devotion.

I still marvel at Naipaul; at the assured humour of the nervous freelance ('a depressed and suppliant class') who in the 1950s set down 'on smooth, non-rustle BBC script paper' the first sentence of his first publishable book.

The loving tenderness of *Miguel Street* – evident in the story of a carpenter who makes a thing without a name – always enthralled my children as I read to them at bedtime.

Sometimes, as a black man, it felt like a betrayal to read him

A few books into his career, though, Naipaul's prose seemed to become more acidic. Sometimes, as a black man, it felt like a betrayal to read him. But Naipaul has always been a guilty pleasure, especially when adopting the provocative jousting of Trinidadian *picong*, or banter. At the start of *The Middle Passage*, he wrote: 'There was such a crowd of immigrant-type West Indians on the boat-train platform at Waterloo that I was glad I was travelling first class.'

It was no consolation that he also turned his eviscerating gaze on the Caribbean's Hindu populations. 'My Aunt Gold Teeth', the story of a wealthy relative who exchanged her sound teeth for 16 gold ones 'to announce to the world that her husband was a man of substance', read both as caricature and truth.

Some pathology, though, was surely on display in the *The Middle Passage,* where Naipaul concluded that in post-independence Caribbean societies the descendants of enslaved Africans and indentured Indians were left to argue among themselves like 'monkeys pleading for evolution'. Naipaul pushed beyond Graham Greene's counsel to write with a sliver of ice in the heart; he dissected his characters with a scalpel.

Even though I increasingly winced at Naipaul's sneering, I recognised its source in the antipathy that kith can feel for kin; Naipaul was Trinidad's recalcitrant prodigal son, whose rejection of his homeland deeply hurt his compatriots and whose affection they most craved.

When snobbery gave way to near celebration

I defended Naipaul. Didn't they recall how funny Naipaul could be? His comedy would return, I argued, as would his humanity. And in part it did. The Brahmin's snobbery and defeated gloom of *India: A Wounded Civilization* lifted and gave way to the near celebratory *India: A Million Mutinies Now*. Inevitably with time, my defence became less forceful. Still though I might bend away from Naipaul I would not break with him.

Twelve years ago at the BBC, I contemplated how I might damage V. S. Naipaul's fedora without being detected. Emerging from the studio he thanked me with such disarming grace I feared he'd read my intentions. When Naipaul reached for the fedora I did not let go of it immediately. In that moment I wanted him to know that despite all the writing of 'ill-made Negroes' I had remained in his corner. Here was the evidence: I had held his hat – and it was intact.

Note on the contributor

Colin Grant's books include *Negro with a Hat: The Rise and Fall of Marcus Garvey* and *Bageye at the Wheel,* short-listed for the PEN/Ackerley prize 2013. His next book, *Homecoming: Voices off Caribbean Migration to Britain*, will be published in 2019. This article first appeared at https://www.theguardian.com/books/2018/aug/18/vs-naipaul-colin-grant-champion-immigrants-children.

Acknowledgements

Every attempt has been made to secure permission to use copyright material. If any proper acknowledgement has not been given, we would invite copyright holders to inform us of the oversight.

Chapter 2, "The futility of human effort — the key Naipaulian preoccupation", by Kenneth Ramchand, first appeared as an obituary in the *Guardian*.

Chapter 3, "Vidia — and the lonely child amidst all the bustle of busy roads", by Paul Theroux, first appeared in the *New York Times*. https://www.newyorker.com/culture/personal-history/memories-of-v-s-naipaul as "Memories of V. S. Naipaul" by Paul Theroux. Copyright © Paul Theroux, 2018, used by permission of The Wylie Agency (UK) Limited.

Chapter 4, "In Sir Vidia's shadow: out of historical darkness", by Clem Seecharan is drawn from his *Finding Myself: Essays on Race, Politics and Culture* (Leeds: Peepal Tree Press, 2015).

Chapter 6, "He was the all-seeing, inner eye that witnessed inconvenient truths", by Sir Hilary Beckles, first appeared at https://www.mona.uwi.edu/marcom/newsroom/entry/7086.

Chapter 7, "Mr. Ford's hacienda", by Tariq Ali, first appeared at https://www.lrb.co.uk/blog/2018/08/13/tariq-ali/mr-fords-hacienda/.

Chapter 9, "The great, frustrating, hilarious Trinidadian showed what we can be in the world", by Kirk Meighoo, was first published at http://www.icdn.today/post/v.s.-naipaul-the-great-frustrating-hilarious-trinidadian-showed-what-we-can-be-in-the-world.

Chapter 10, "Scientist as well as artist", by Lloyd Best, was first published in the *Trinidad and Tobago Review*, Vol. 23, Nos 9-10.

Chapter 11, "The sense of historical wonder never left him", by Bridget Brereton. first appeared at https://www.trinidadexpress.com.

Chapter 12, "His world was what it was: the enigma of V. S. Naipaul", by Nicholas Laughlin, was first published at https://globalvoices.org/2018/08/12/his-world-was-what-it-was-the-enigma-of-v-s-naipaul/.

Chapter 14, "He was easily the most difficult writer I've ever worked with", by Diana Athill, first appeared in the *Guardian* at https://www.theguardian.com/books/2018/aug/17/diana-athill-vs-naipaul-delighted-stories.

Chapter 15, "The mimic man supreme", by Jug Suraiya, first appeared at https://blogs.timesofindia.indiatimes.com/jugglebandhi/vs-naipaul-nowhere-man/.

Chapter 16, "Thirteen times Naipaul stirred the pot of controversy with objectionable statements", by Urvashi Bahuguna, first appeared at https://scroll.in/article/890932/thirteen-times-vs-naipaul-stirred-the-pot-of-controversy-with-objectionable-statements.

Chapter 18, "Reflecting on the good and the bad of the man", by Narissa Deokarran is based on her letter which appeared at https://www.stabroeknews.com/2018/opinion/letters/08/22/reflect-on-the-good-and-the-bad.

Chapter 19, "An intellectual catastrophe", by Edward Said, ©copyright *Al-Ahram Weekly* was originally published in the issue dated 6-12 August 1998.

Chapter 20, "How he treated his critics: with silence bordering on disdain", by Anil Dharker, first appeared at https://timesofindia.indiatimes.com/vs-naipaul/vs-naipaul-a-visit-to-banganga-was-his-only-request/articleshow/65380346.cms?

Chapter 21, "His gentle side", by Ahsan Akbar, first appeared at https://www.spectator.co.uk/2018/08/v-s-naipauls-gentle-side/.

Chapter 22, "When Sir Vidia held out his fedora – and gave it me to hold…", by Colin Grant, first appeared at https://www.theguardian.com/books/2018/aug/18/vs-naipaul-colin-grant-champion-immigrants-children.

Bite-Sized Lifestyle Books are designed to provide insights and ideas about our lives, our interests and the pressures on all of us and what we can do to appreciate and change our environment and ourselves.

They are deliberately short, easy to read, books helping readers to gain a different perspective. They are firmly based on personal experience and look to enhance the human spirit.

The most successful people all share an ability to focus on what really matters, keeping things simple and understandable. As Stephen Covey famously said, "The main thing is to keep the main thing, the main thing".

But what exactly is the main thing?

Bite-Sized Books were conceived to help answer precisely that question crisply and fast and, of course, be engaging to read, written by people who are experienced and successful in their field.

The brief? Distil the *main things* into a book that can be read by an intelligent non-expert comfortably in around 60 minutes. Make sure the book enables the reader with specific ideas and plenty of examples drawn from real life. In some cases the books are a virtual mentor.

Bite-Sized Books don't cover every eventuality, but they are written from the heart by successful people who are happy to share their experience with you and give you the benefit of their success, while celebrating achievements with an optimistic outlook.

We have avoided jargon – or explained it where we have used it as a shorthand – and made few assumptions about the reader, except that they are literate and numerate, and that they can adapt and use what we suggest to suit their own, individual purposes.

They can be read straight through at one easy sitting and then used as a support while you are thinking further about the issues that most of us face.

Bite-Sized Books Catalogue

Business Books

Lifestyle Books

Bill Heine
    Cancer – Living Behind Enemy Lines Without a Map
Regina Kerschbaumer
    Yoga Coffee and a Glass of Wine
        A Yoga Journey
Gillian Perry
    Capturing the Celestial Lights
        A Practical Guide to Imagining the Northern Lights
Arthur Worrell
    A Grandfather's Story
        Arthur Worrell's War

Public Affairs Books

Eben Black
    Lies Lunch and Lobbying
        PR, Public Affairs and Political Engagement – A Guide
John Mair and Richard Keeble (Editors)
    Investigative Journalism Today:
        Speaking Truth to Power
John Mair, Richard Keeble and Farrukh Dhondy (Editors)
    V.S Naipaul:
        The legacy
Christian Wolmar
    Wolmar for London
        Creating a Grassroots Campaign in a Digital Age

Printed in Great Britain
by Amazon

56720129R00079